# THE COLLECTED WORKS of TONY MILLIONAIRE'S

# Sock Monkey

## VOLUMES THREE and FOUR

For
**Ann-Louise**

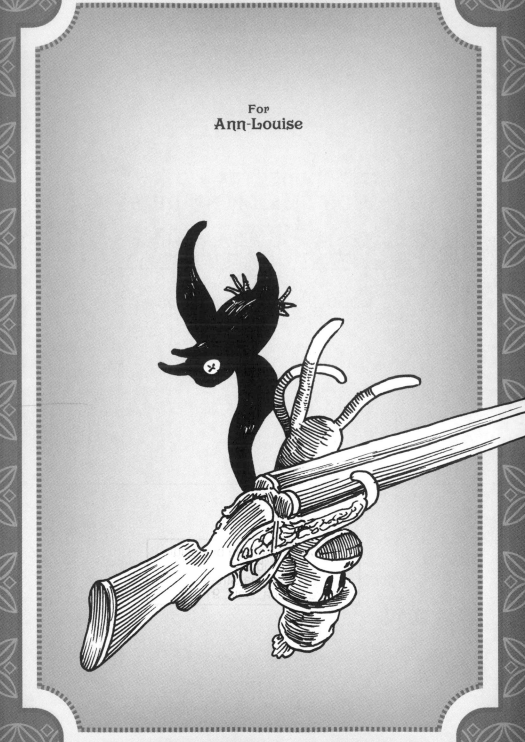

# THE COLLECTED WORKS
## of TONY MILLIONAIRE'S

SOC MONKEY

written and drawn by
## Tony Millionaire

### VOLUMES THREE and FOUR

TM
**Dark Horse Books**

EDITOR
**Dave Land**

BOOK DESIGN
**Lia Ribacchi**

PUBLISHER
**Mike Richardson**

THE COLLECTED WORKS OF
TONY MILLIONAIRE'S SOCK MONKEY™
VOLUMES THREE & FOUR

This book collects Volume Three, issues #1-2, and Volume
Four, issues #1-2, of the Dark Horse comic book series
Tony Millionaire's Sock Monkey™.

Dark Horse Books
A division of Dark Horse Comics, Inc.
10956 SE Main Street
Milwaukie, OR 97222

www.darkhorse.com

To find a comic shop in your area
call the Comic Shop Locator Service: (888) 266-4226

First edition: January 2004
ISBN: 1-59307-098-5

1 3 5 7 9 10 8 6 4 2

Printed in Canada

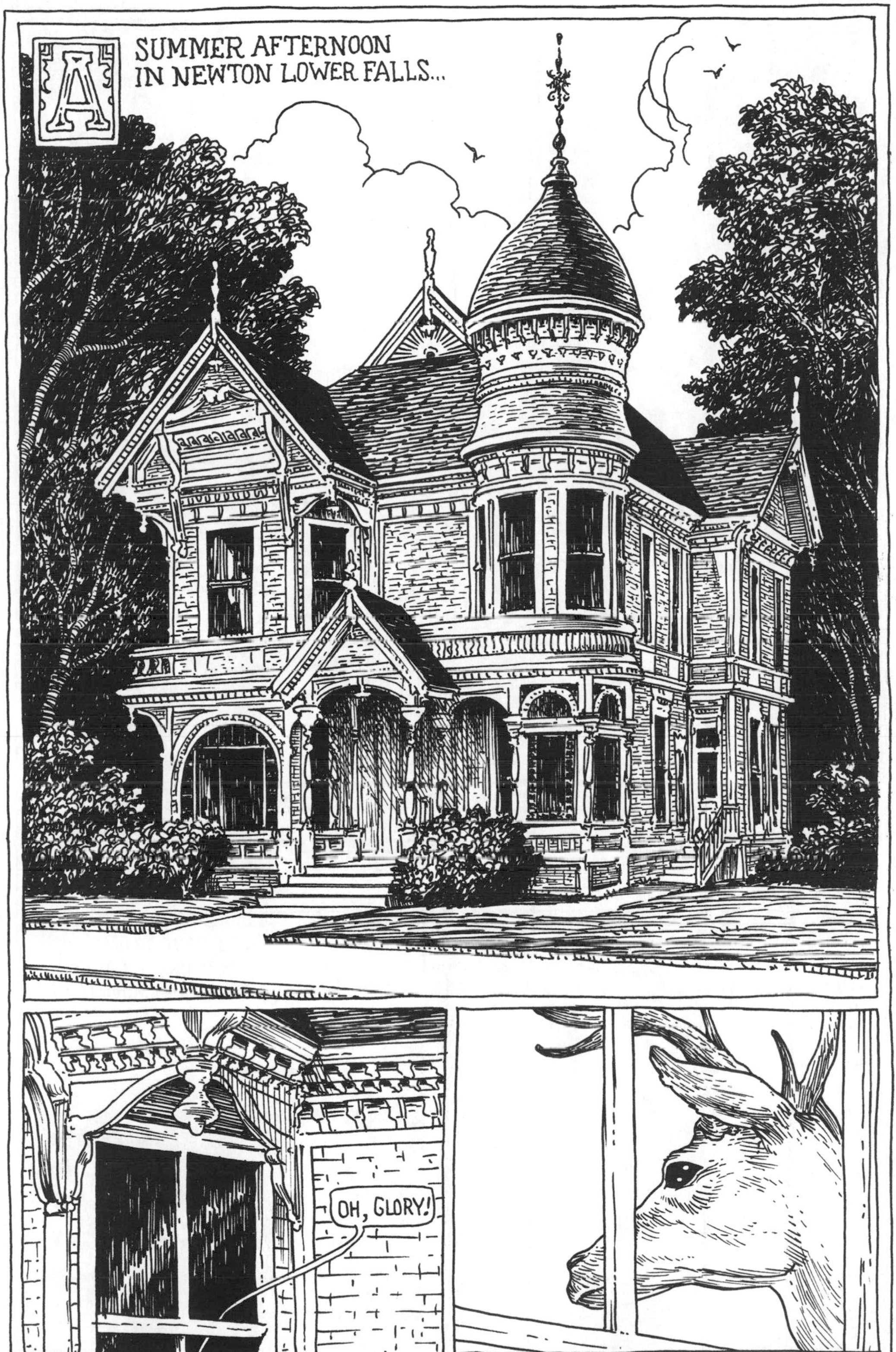
A SUMMER AFTERNOON IN NEWTON LOWER FALLS...
OH, GLORY!

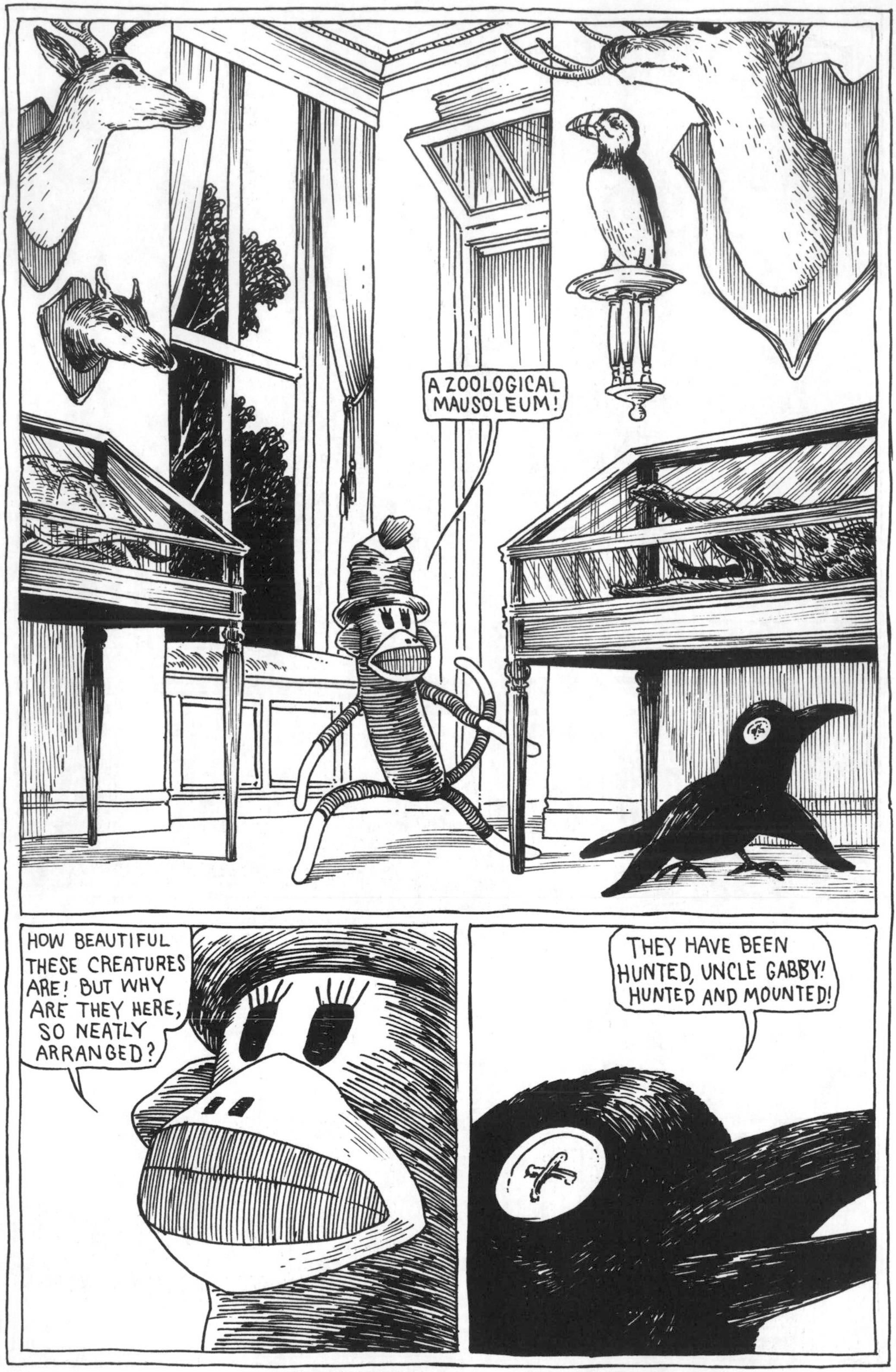
A ZOOLOGICAL MAUSOLEUM!
HOW BEAUTIFUL THESE CREATURES ARE! BUT WHY ARE THEY HERE, SO NEATLY ARRANGED?
THEY HAVE BEEN HUNTED, UNCLE GABBY! HUNTED AND MOUNTED!

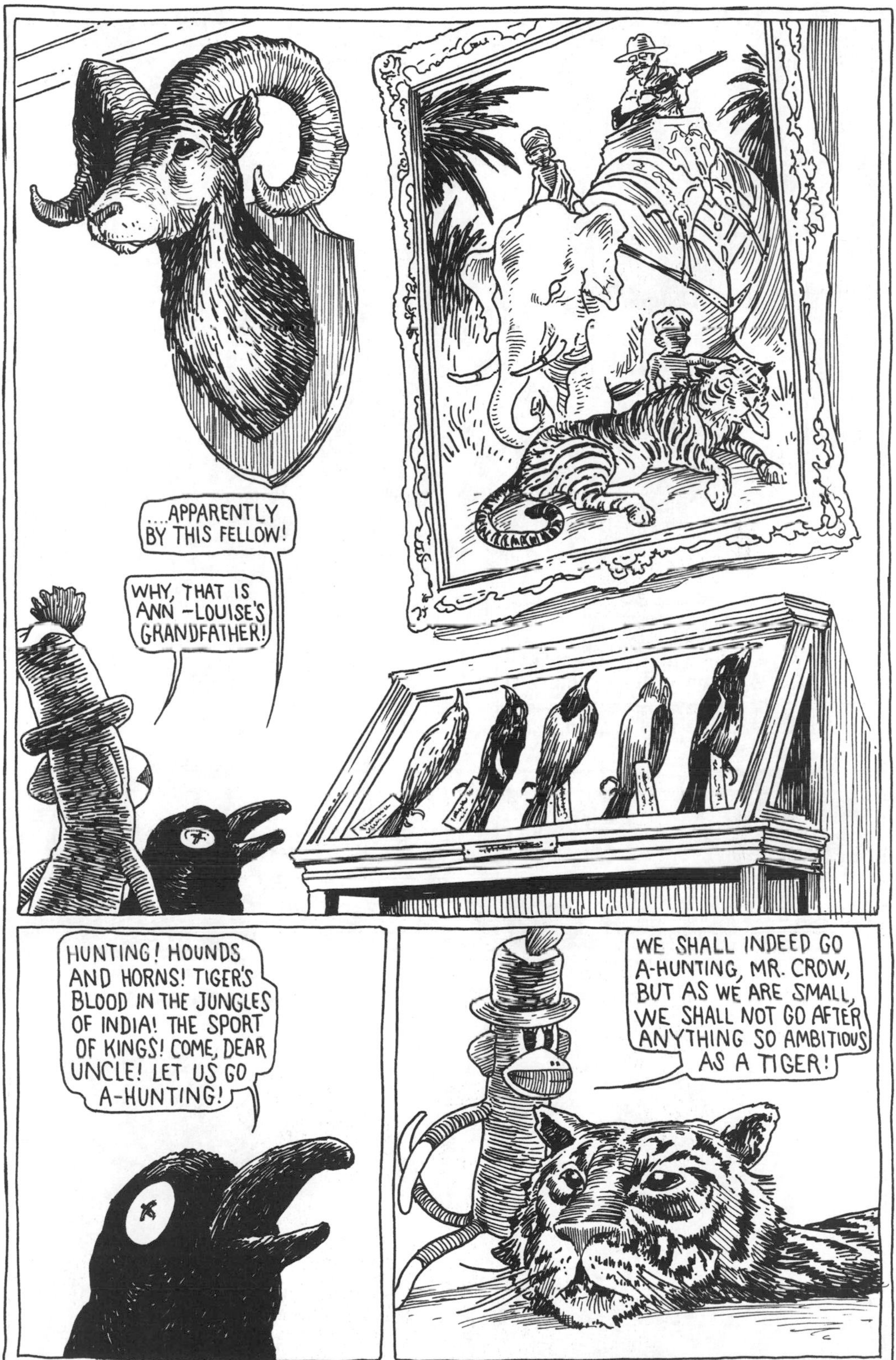
....APPARENTLY BY THIS FELLOW!
WHY, THAT IS ANN -LOUISE'S GRANDFATHER!
HUNTING! HOUNDS AND HORNS! TIGER'S BLOOD IN THE JUNGLES OF INDIA! THE SPORT OF KINGS! COME, DEAR UNCLE! LET US GO A-HUNTING!
WE SHALL INDEED GO A-HUNTING, MR. CROW, BUT AS WE ARE SMALL, WE SHALL NOT GO AFTER ANYTHING SO AMBITIOUS AS A TIGER!

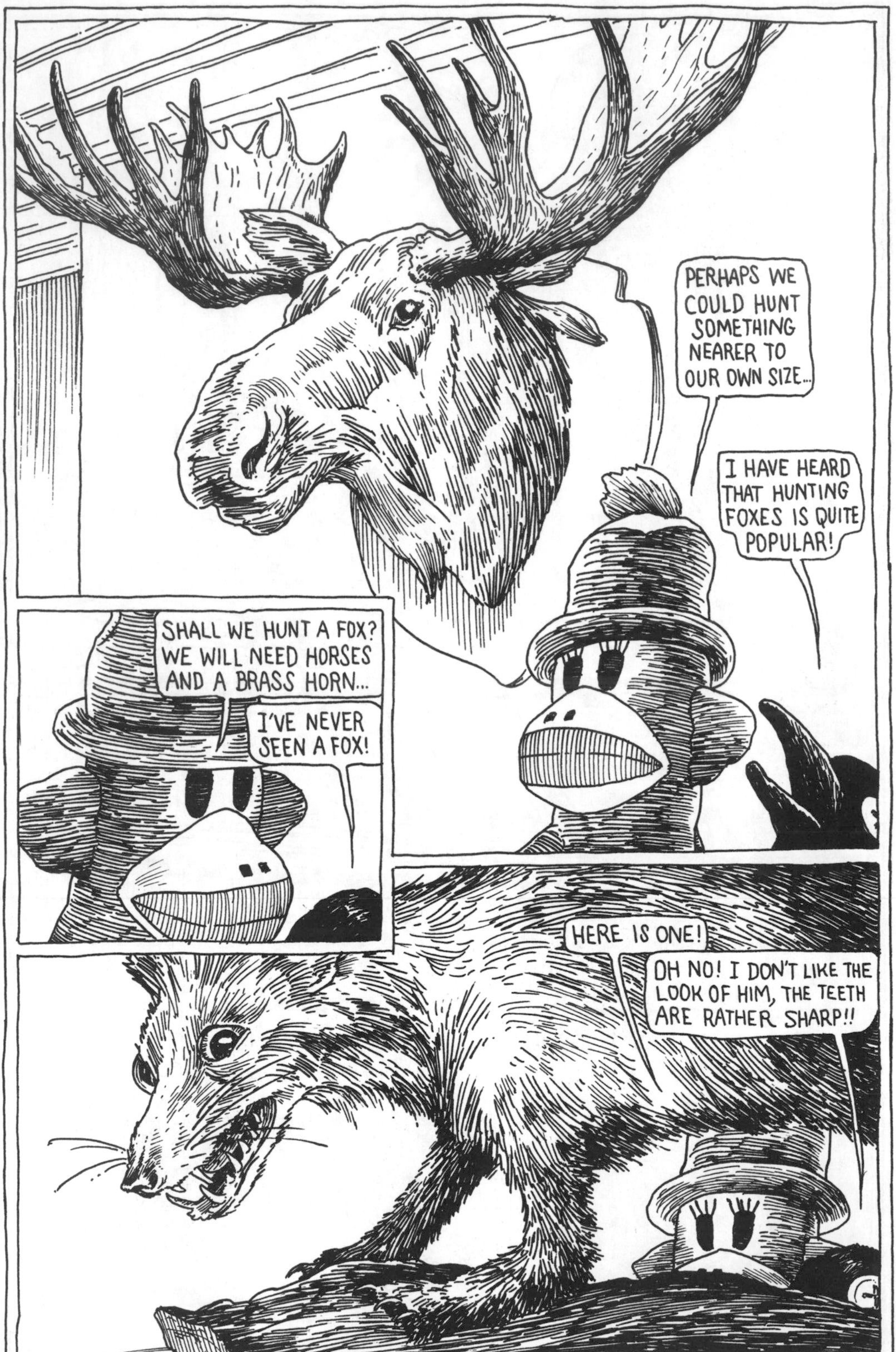
PERHAPS WE COULD HUNT SOMETHING NEARER TO OUR OWN SIZE...
I HAVE HEARD THAT HUNTING FOXES IS QUITE POPULAR!
SHALL WE HUNT A FOX? WE WILL NEED HORSES AND A BRASS HORN...
I'VE NEVER SEEN A FOX!
HERE IS ONE!
OH NO! I DON'T LIKE THE LOOK OF HIM, THE TEETH ARE RATHER SHARP!!

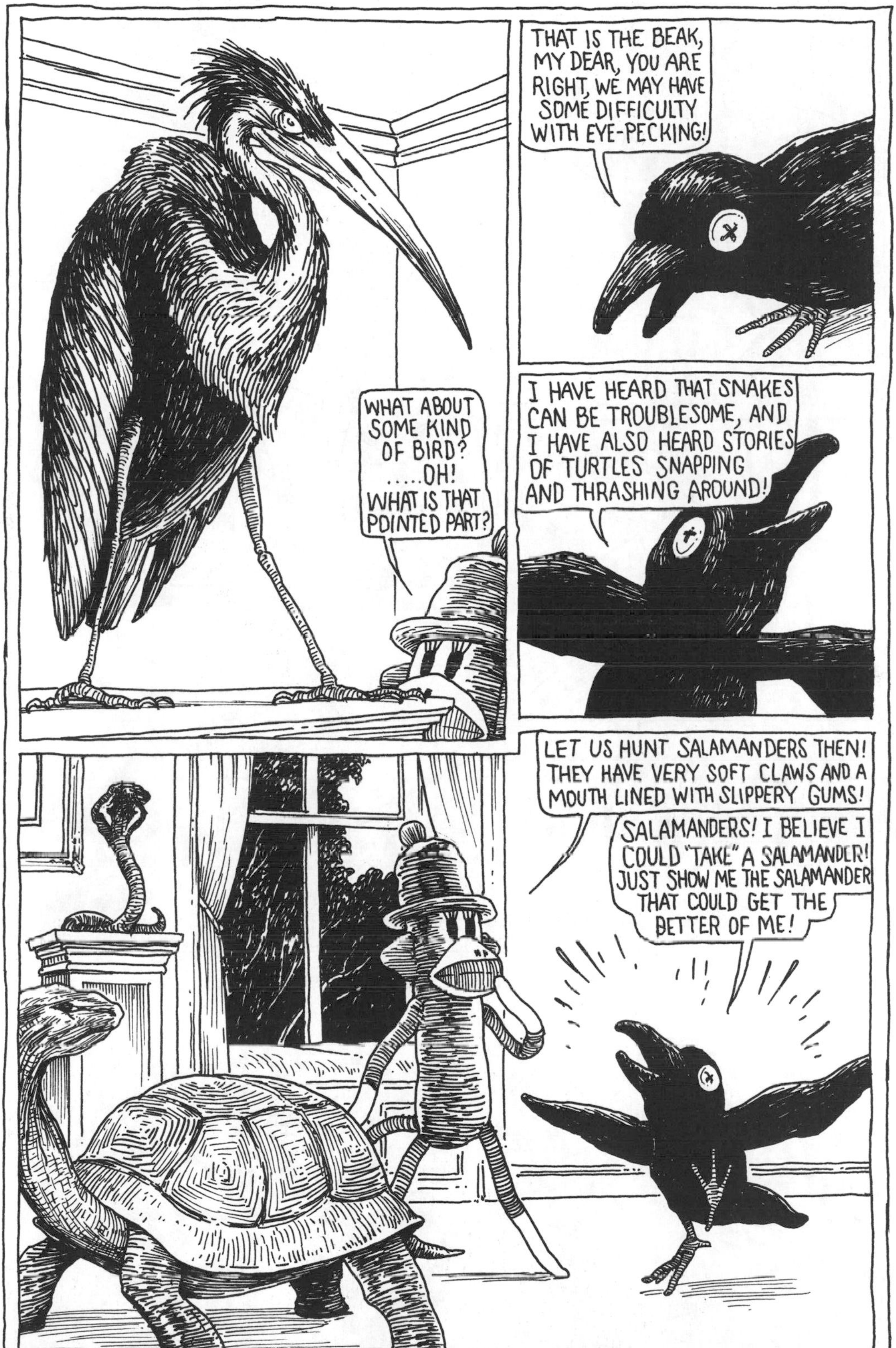
THAT IS THE BEAK, MY DEAR, YOU ARE RIGHT, WE MAY HAVE SOME DIFFICULTY WITH EYE-PECKING!
WHAT ABOUT SOME KIND OF BIRD? .....OH! WHAT IS THAT POINTED PART?
I HAVE HEARD THAT SNAKES CAN BE TROUBLESOME, AND I HAVE ALSO HEARD STORIES OF TURTLES SNAPPING AND THRASHING AROUND!
LET US HUNT SALAMANDERS THEN! THEY HAVE VERY SOFT CLAWS AND A MOUTH LINED WITH SLIPPERY GUMS!
SALAMANDERS! I BELIEVE I COULD "TAKE" A SALAMANDER! JUST SHOW ME THE SALAMANDER THAT COULD GET THE BETTER OF ME!

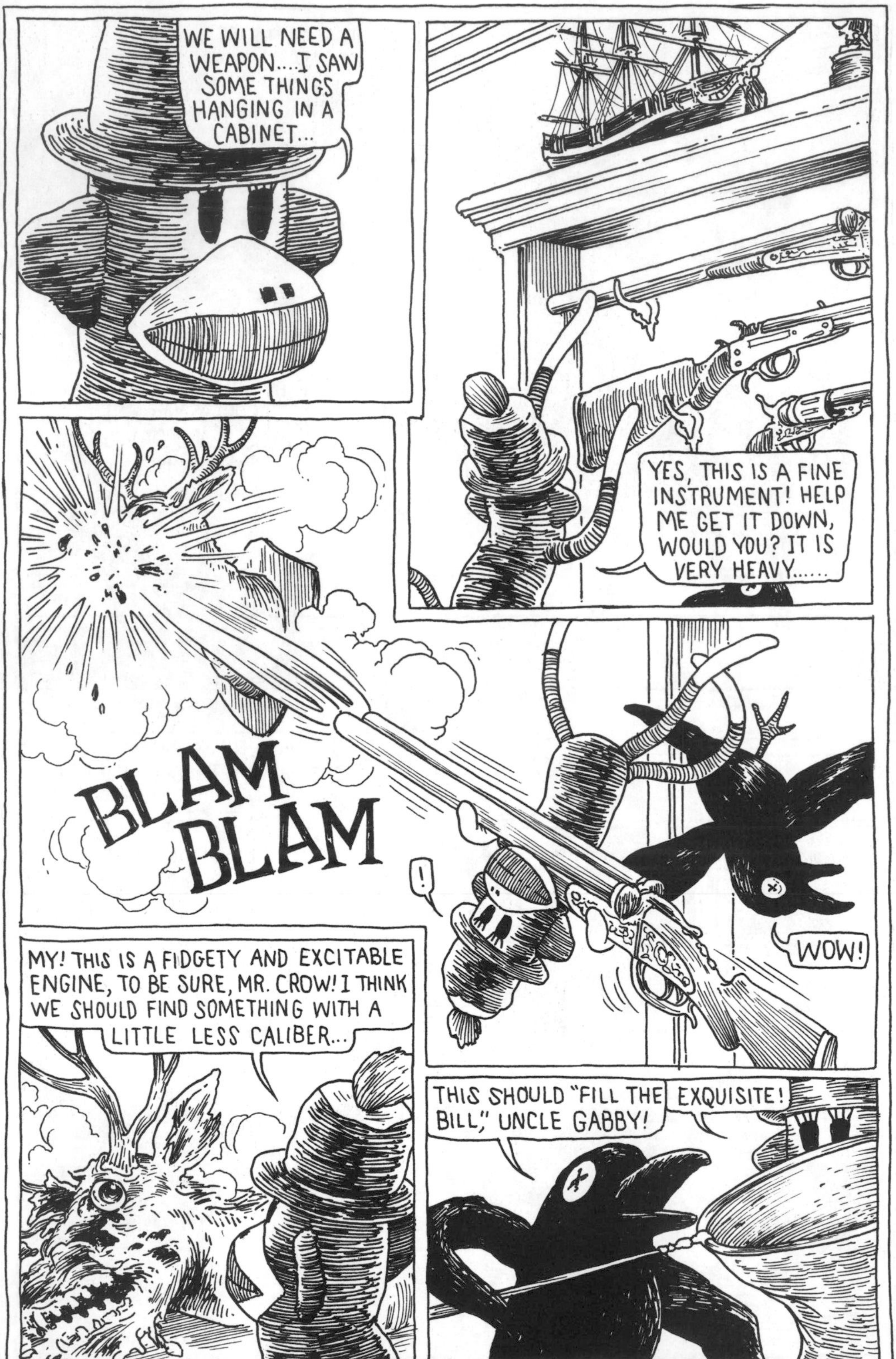
WE WILL NEED A WEAPON....I SAW SOME THINGS HANGING IN A CABINET...
YES, THIS IS A FINE INSTRUMENT! HELP ME GET IT DOWN, WOULD YOU? IT IS VERY HEAVY......
BLAM
BLAM
!
WOW!
MY! THIS IS A FIDGETY AND EXCITABLE ENGINE, TO BE SURE, MR. CROW! I THINK WE SHOULD FIND SOMETHING WITH A LITTLE LESS CALIBER...
THIS SHOULD "FILL THE BILL," UNCLE GABBY!
EXQUISITE!

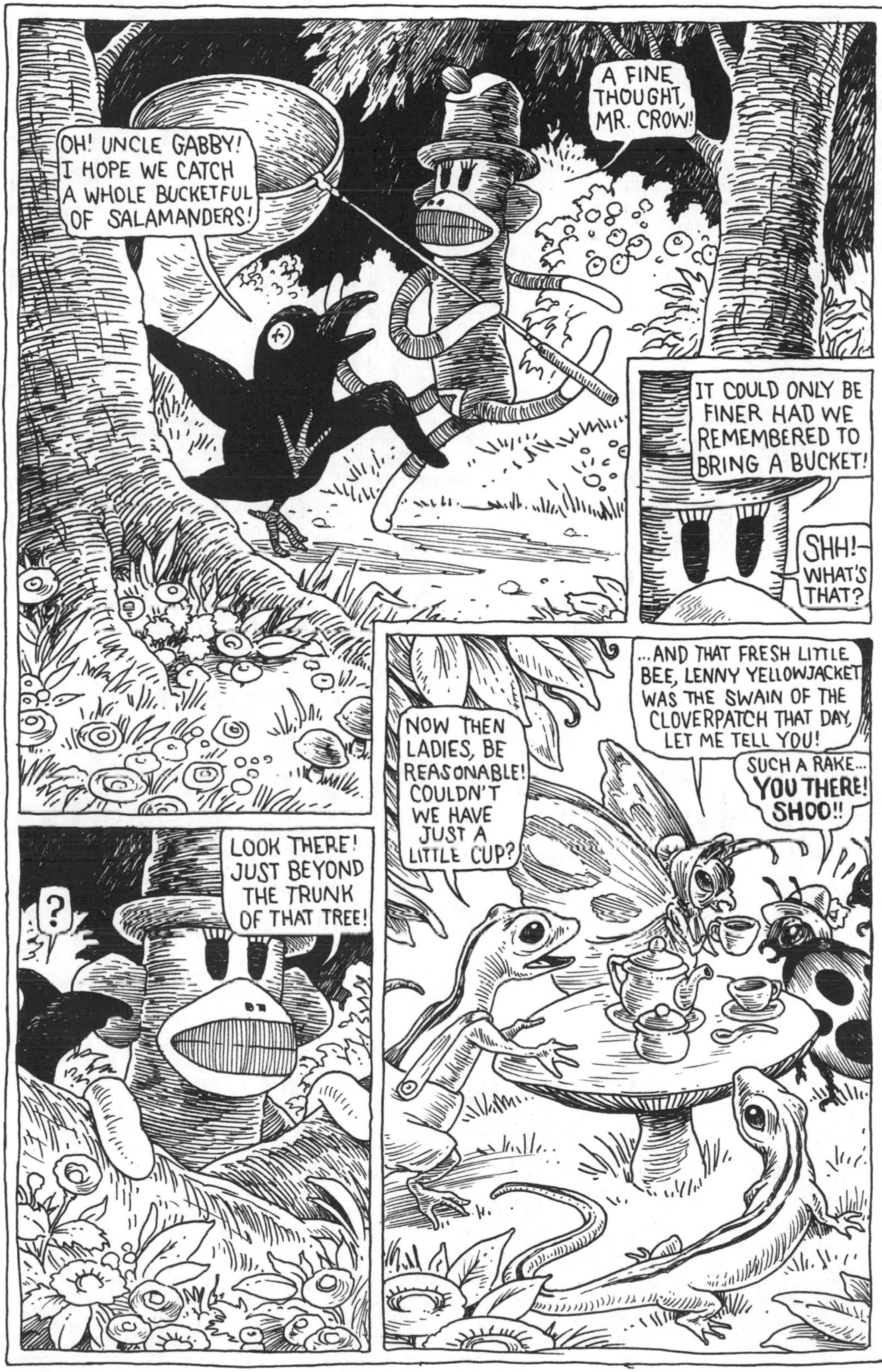
OH! UNCLE GABBY! I HOPE WE CATCH A WHOLE BUCKETFUL OF SALAMANDERS!
A FINE THOUGHT, MR. CROW!
IT COULD ONLY BE FINER HAD WE REMEMBERED TO BRING A BUCKET!
SHH!— WHAT'S THAT?
?
LOOK THERE! JUST BEYOND THE TRUNK OF THAT TREE!
...AND THAT FRESH LITTLE BEE, LENNY YELLOWJACKET WAS THE SWAIN OF THE CLOVERPATCH THAT DAY, LET ME TELL YOU!
NOW THEN LADIES, BE REASONABLE! COULDN'T WE HAVE JUST A LITTLE CUP?
SUCH A RAKE... YOU THERE! SHOO!!

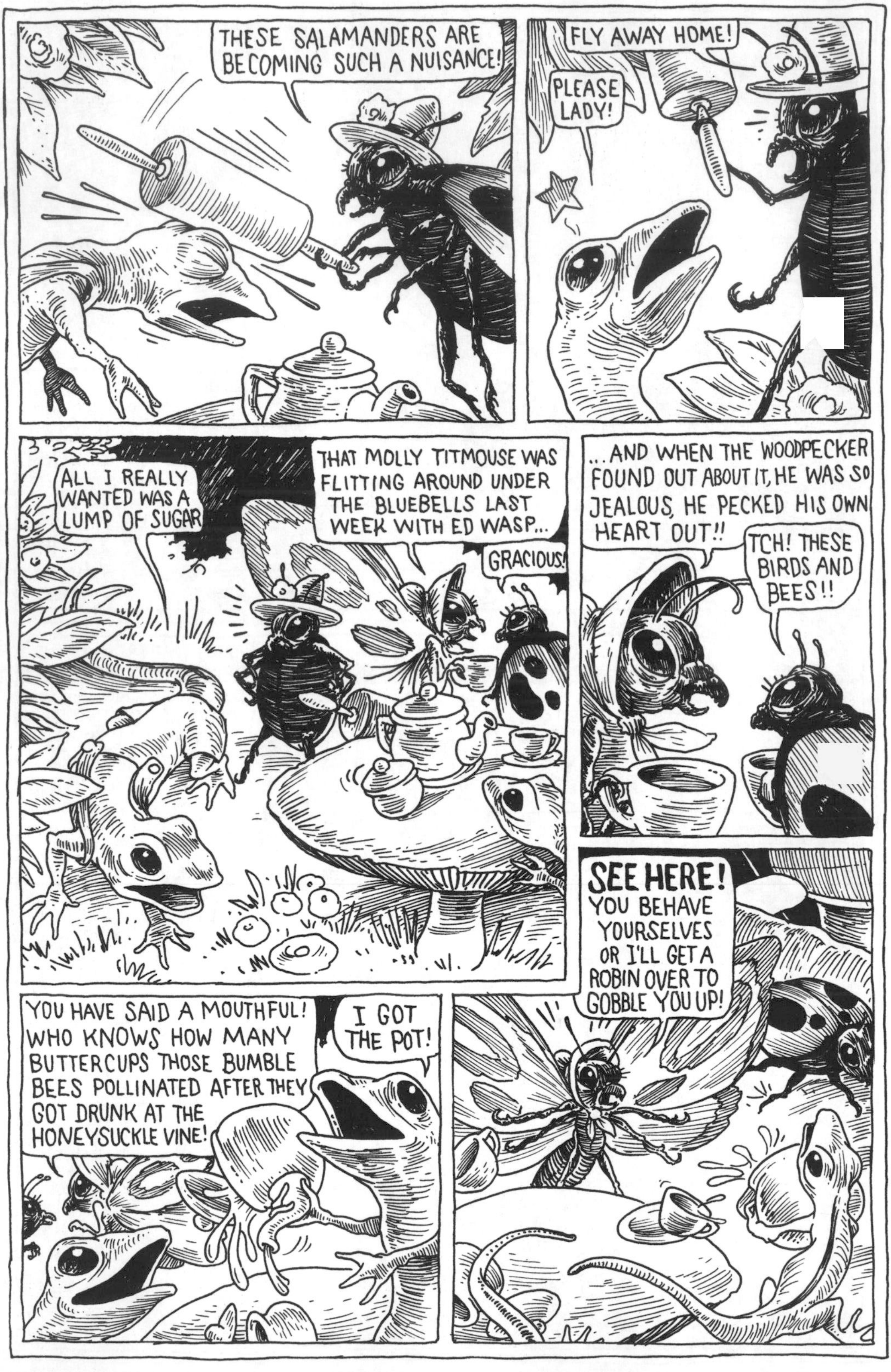

THESE SALAMANDERS ARE BECOMING SUCH A NUISANCE!
FLY AWAY HOME!
PLEASE LADY!
ALL I REALLY WANTED WAS A LUMP OF SUGAR
THAT MOLLY TITMOUSE WAS FLITTING AROUND UNDER THE BLUEBELLS LAST WEEK WITH ED WASP...
GRACIOUS!
...AND WHEN THE WOODPECKER FOUND OUT ABOUT IT, HE WAS SO JEALOUS, HE PECKED HIS OWN HEART OUT!!
TCH! THESE BIRDS AND BEES!!
YOU HAVE SAID A MOUTHFUL! WHO KNOWS HOW MANY BUTTERCUPS THOSE BUMBLE BEES POLLINATED AFTER THEY GOT DRUNK AT THE HONEYSUCKLE VINE!
I GOT THE POT!
SEE HERE! YOU BEHAVE YOURSELVES OR I'LL GET A ROBIN OVER TO GOBBLE YOU UP!

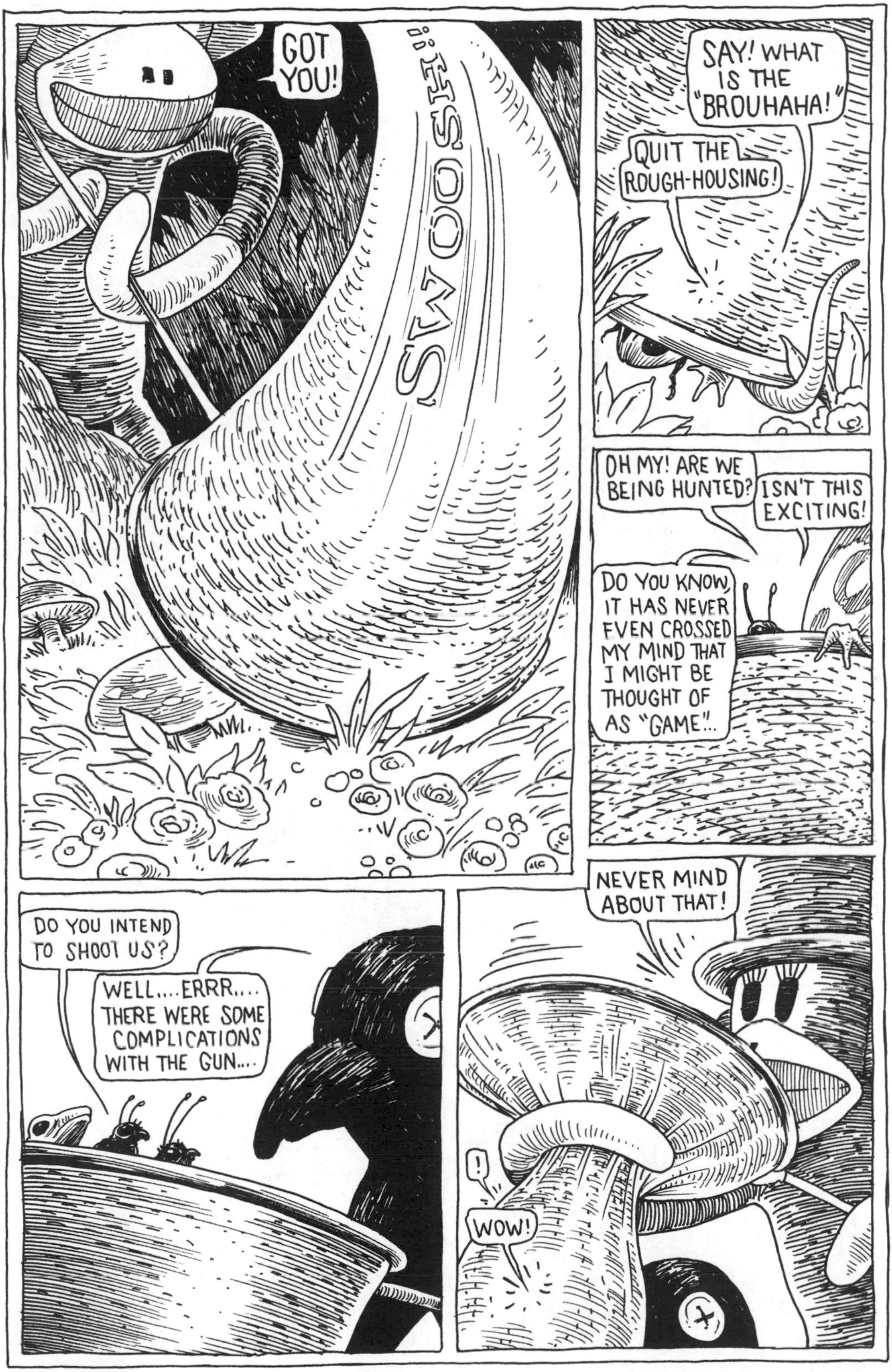
GOT YOU!
SWOOSH!!!
SAY! WHAT IS THE "BROUHAHA!"
QUIT THE ROUGH-HOUSING!
OH MY! ARE WE BEING HUNTED?
ISN'T THIS EXCITING!
DO YOU KNOW, IT HAS NEVER EVEN CROSSED MY MIND THAT I MIGHT BE THOUGHT OF AS "GAME"...
DO YOU INTEND TO SHOOT US?
WELL.... ERRR.... THERE WERE SOME COMPLICATIONS WITH THE GUN....
NEVER MIND ABOUT THAT!
!
WOW!

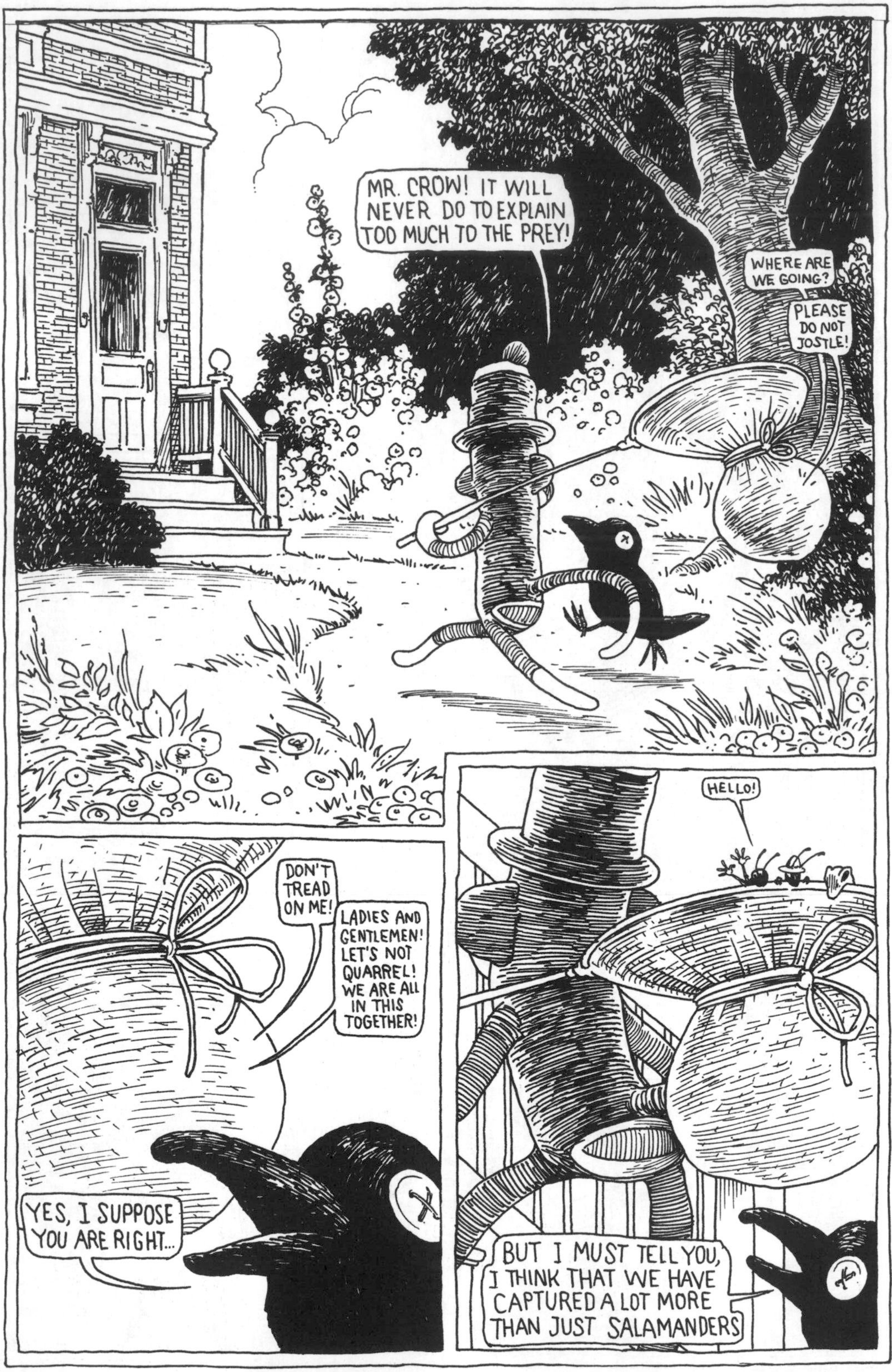
MR. CROW! IT WILL NEVER DO TO EXPLAIN TOO MUCH TO THE PREY!
WHERE ARE WE GOING?
PLEASE DO NOT JOSTLE!
DON'T TREAD ON ME!
LADIES AND GENTLEMEN! LET'S NOT QUARREL! WE ARE ALL IN THIS TOGETHER!
YES, I SUPPOSE YOU ARE RIGHT...
HELLO!
BUT I MUST TELL YOU, I THINK THAT WE HAVE CAPTURED A LOT MORE THAN JUST SALAMANDERS

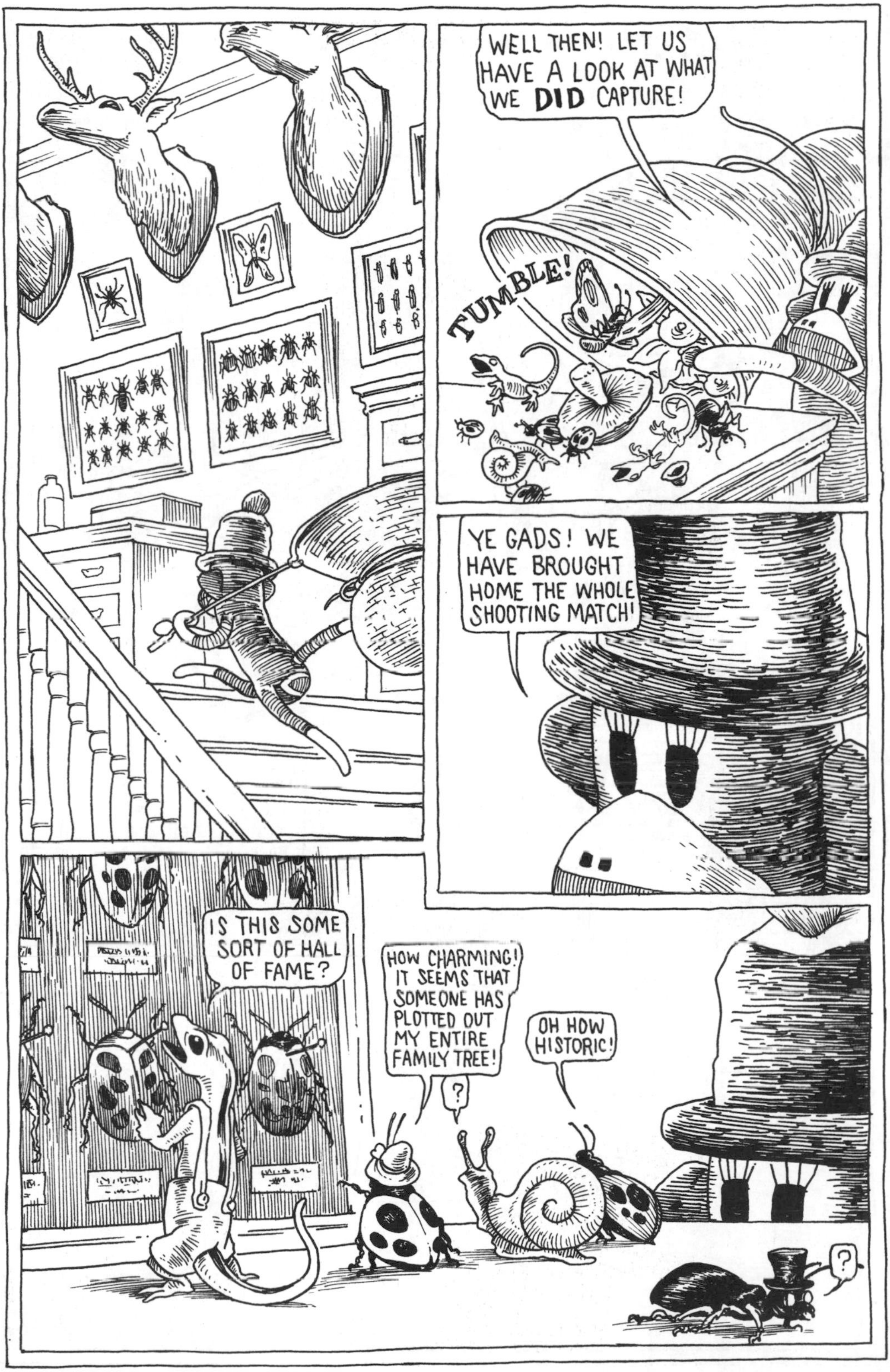
WELL THEN! LET US HAVE A LOOK AT WHAT WE **DID** CAPTURE!
TUMBLE!
YE GADS! WE HAVE BROUGHT HOME THE WHOLE SHOOTING MATCH!
IS THIS SOME SORT OF HALL OF FAME?
HOW CHARMING! IT SEEMS THAT SOMEONE HAS PLOTTED OUT MY ENTIRE FAMILY TREE!
?
OH HOW HISTORIC!
?

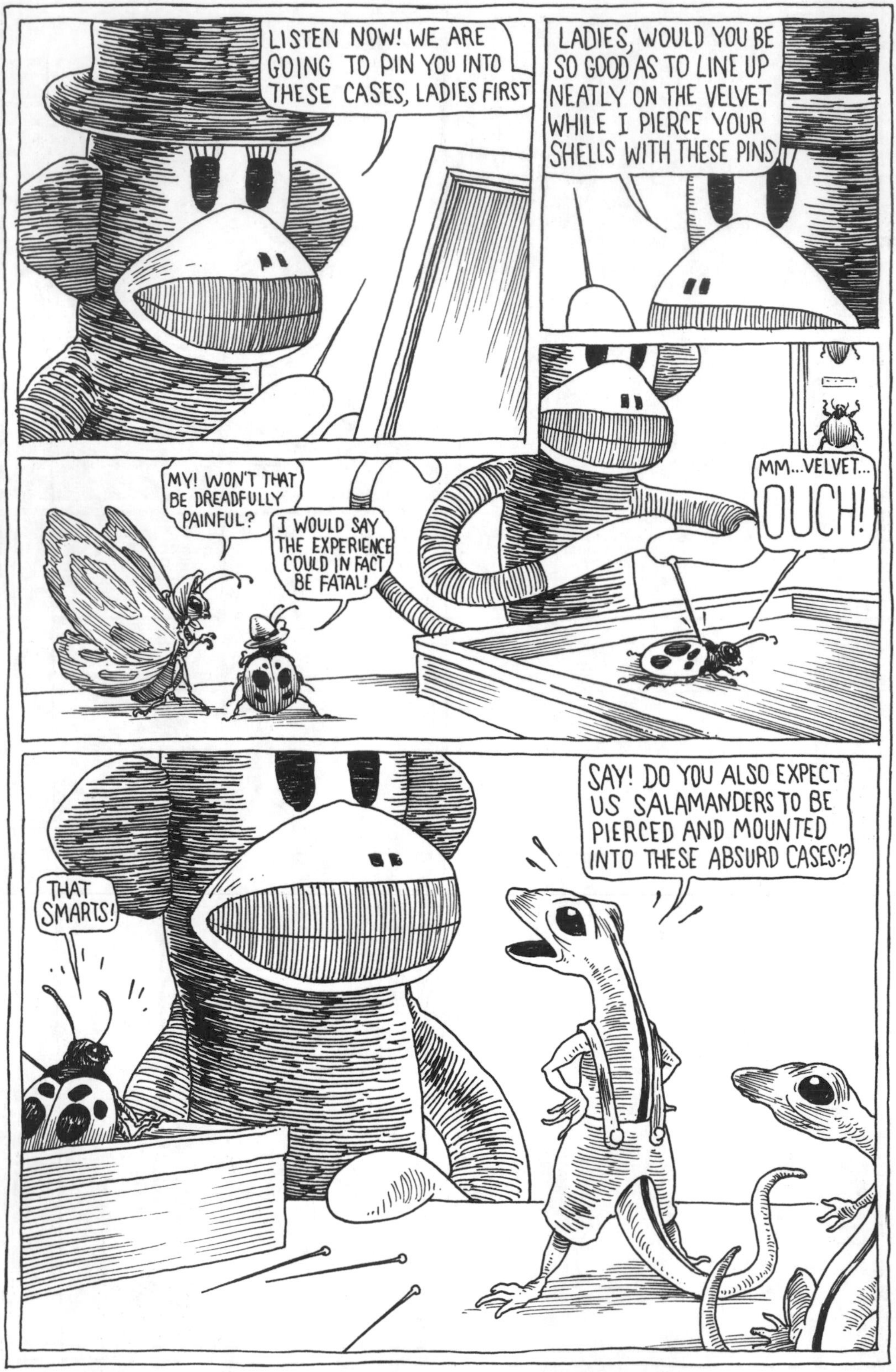
LISTEN NOW! WE ARE GOING TO PIN YOU INTO THESE CASES, LADIES FIRST
LADIES, WOULD YOU BE SO GOOD AS TO LINE UP NEATLY ON THE VELVET WHILE I PIERCE YOUR SHELLS WITH THESE PINS
MY! WON'T THAT BE DREADFULLY PAINFUL?
I WOULD SAY THE EXPERIENCE COULD IN FACT BE FATAL!
MM...VELVET... OUCH!
THAT SMARTS!
SAY! DO YOU ALSO EXPECT US SALAMANDERS TO BE PIERCED AND MOUNTED INTO THESE ABSURD CASES!?

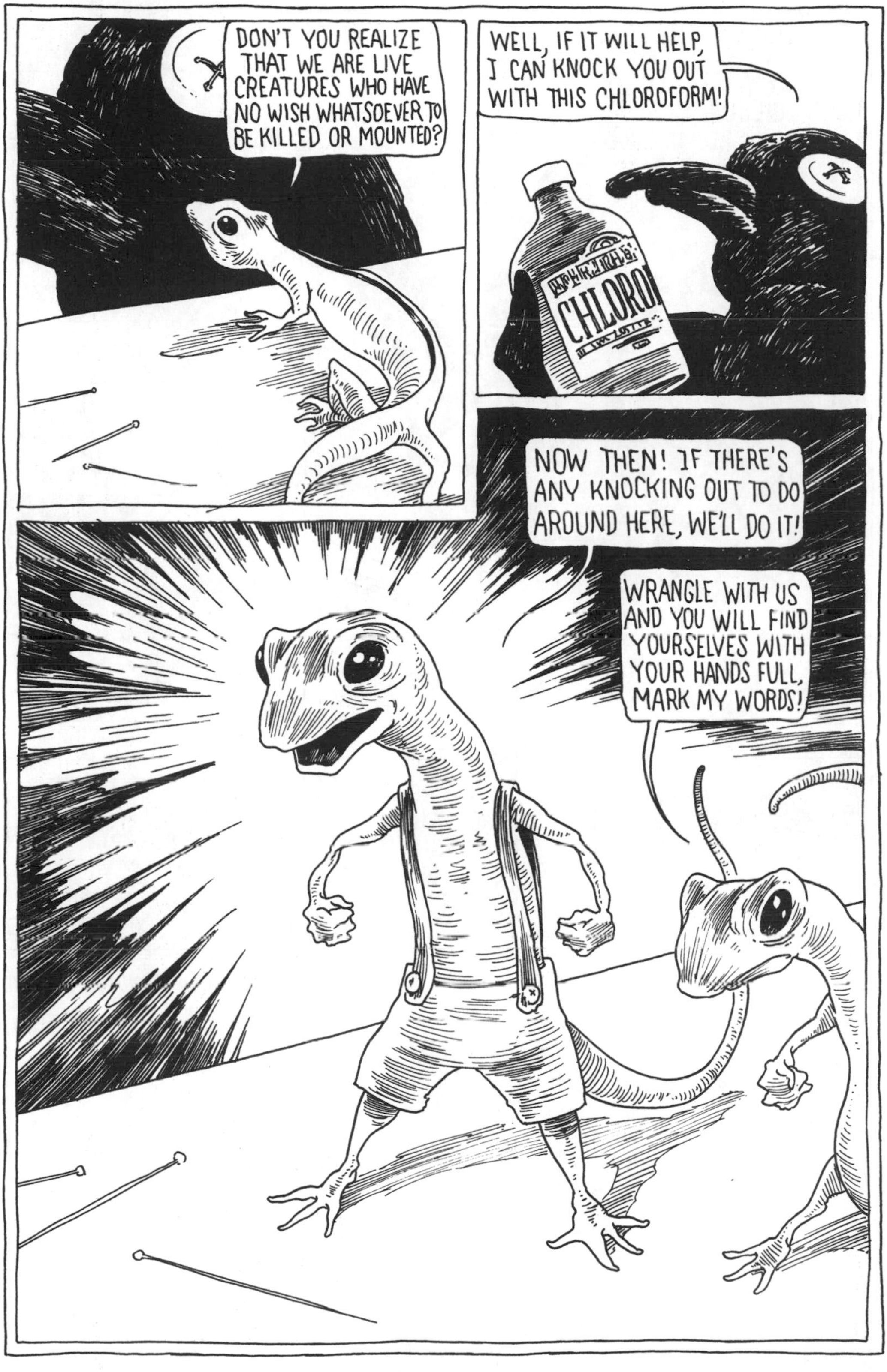
DON'T YOU REALIZE THAT WE ARE LIVE CREATURES WHO HAVE NO WISH WHATSOEVER TO BE KILLED OR MOUNTED?
WELL, IF IT WILL HELP, I CAN KNOCK YOU OUT WITH THIS CHLOROFORM!
CHLORO
NOW THEN! IF THERE'S ANY KNOCKING OUT TO DO AROUND HERE, WE'LL DO IT!
WRANGLE WITH US AND YOU WILL FIND YOURSELVES WITH YOUR HANDS FULL, MARK MY WORDS!

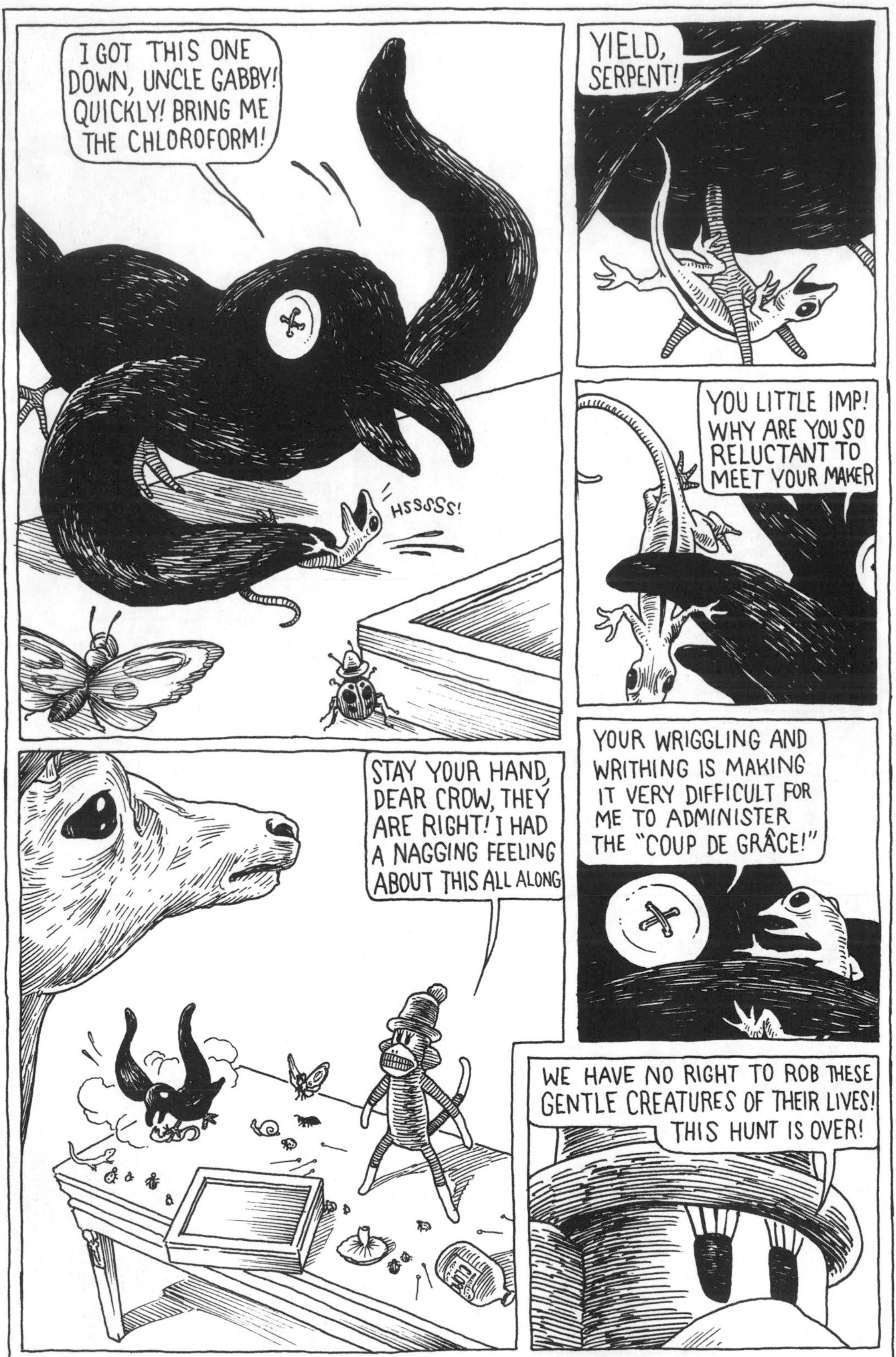
I GOT THIS ONE DOWN, UNCLE GABBY! QUICKLY! BRING ME THE CHLOROFORM!
HSSSSS!
YIELD, SERPENT!
YOU LITTLE IMP! WHY ARE YOU SO RELUCTANT TO MEET YOUR MAKER
STAY YOUR HAND, DEAR CROW, THEY ARE RIGHT! I HAD A NAGGING FEELING ABOUT THIS ALL ALONG
YOUR WRIGGLING AND WRITHING IS MAKING IT VERY DIFFICULT FOR ME TO ADMINISTER THE "COUP DE GRÂCE!"
WE HAVE NO RIGHT TO ROB THESE GENTLE CREATURES OF THEIR LIVES! THIS HUNT IS OVER!

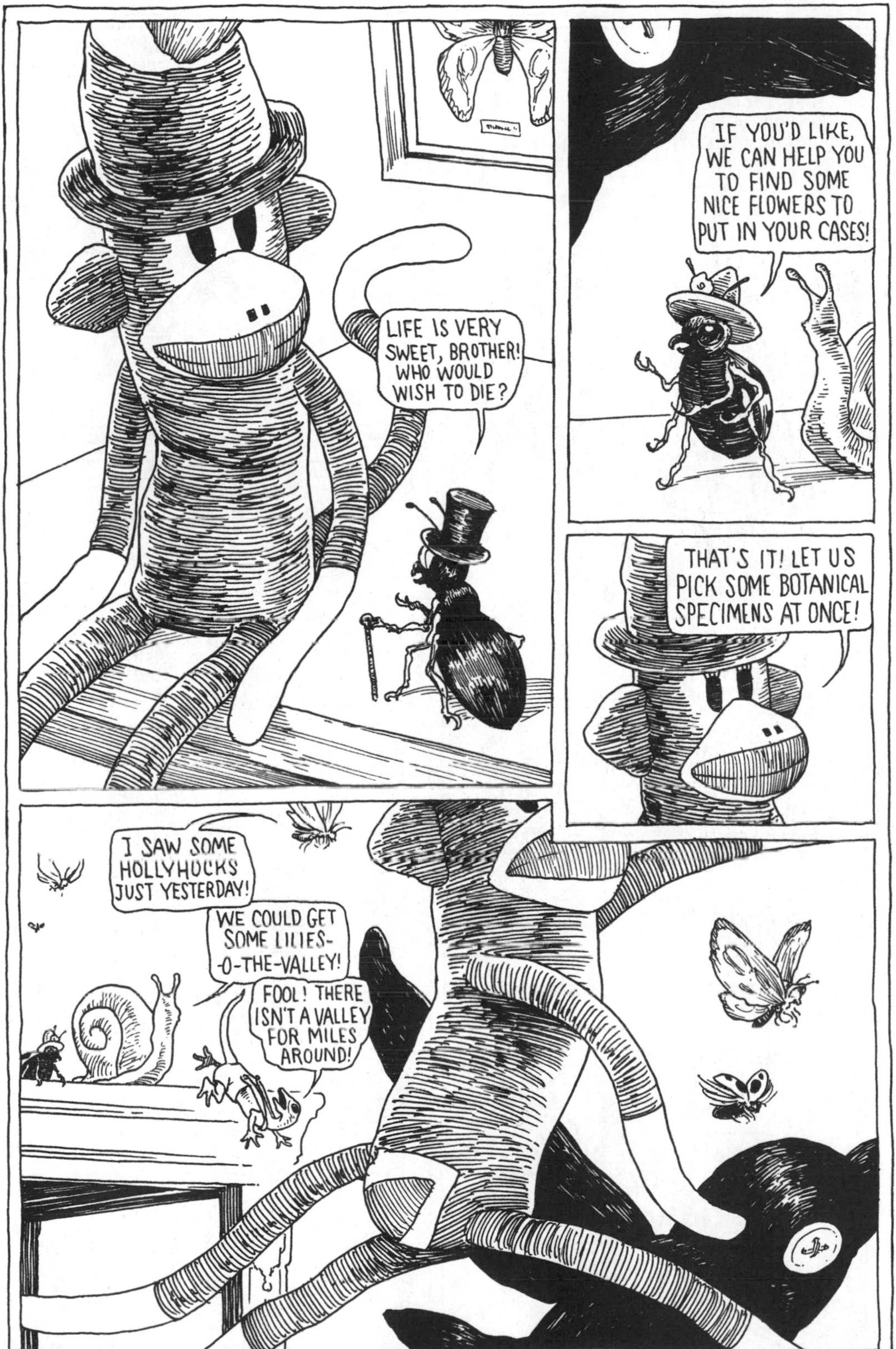
LIFE IS VERY SWEET, BROTHER! WHO WOULD WISH TO DIE?
IF YOU'D LIKE, WE CAN HELP YOU TO FIND SOME NICE FLOWERS TO PUT IN YOUR CASES!
THAT'S IT! LET US PICK SOME BOTANICAL SPECIMENS AT ONCE!
I SAW SOME HOLLYHOCKS JUST YESTERDAY!
WE COULD GET SOME LILIES-O-THE-VALLEY!
FOOL! THERE ISN'T A VALLEY FOR MILES AROUND!

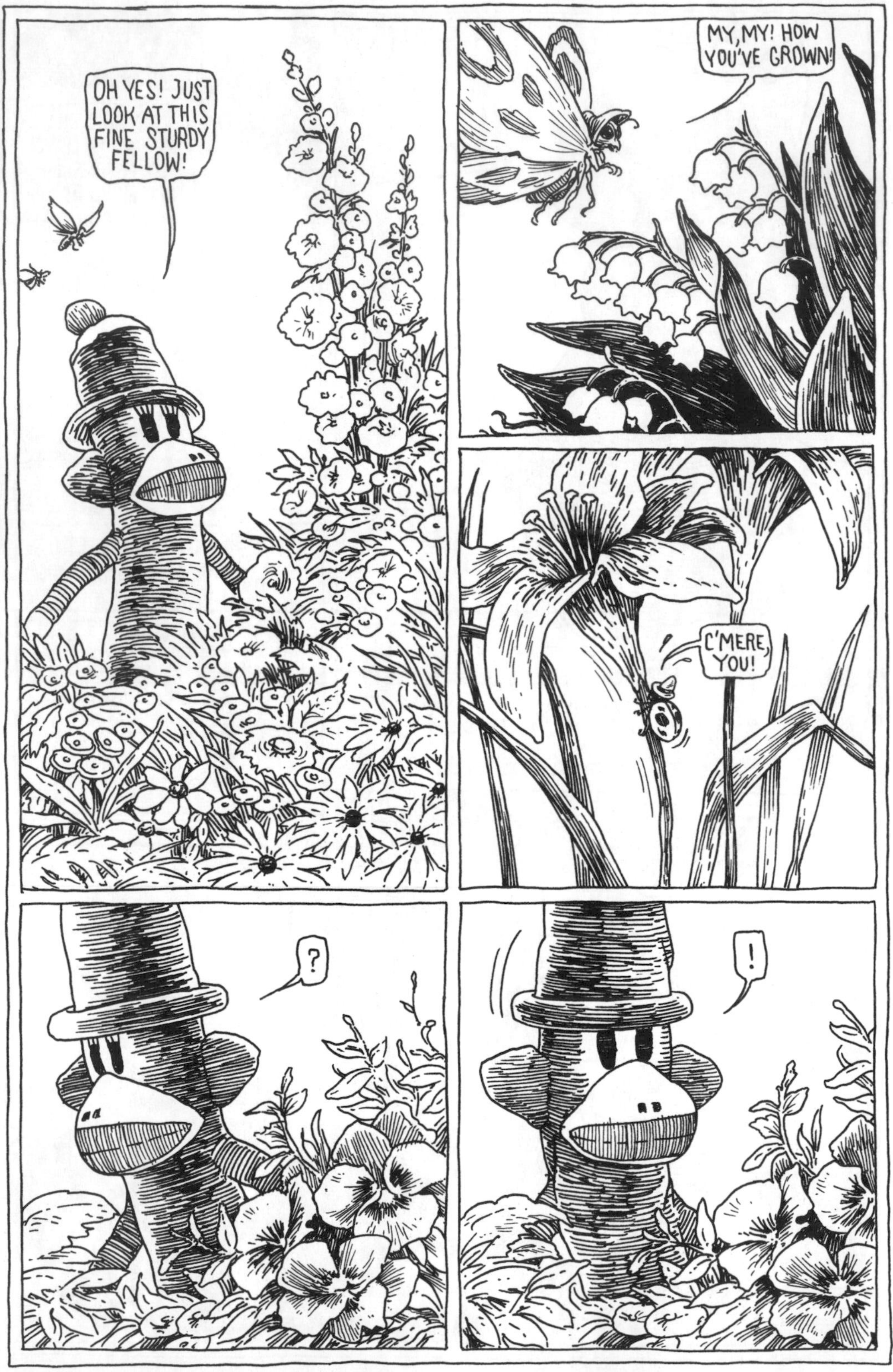
OH YES! JUST LOOK AT THIS FINE STURDY FELLOW!
MY, MY! HOW YOU'VE GROWN!
C'MERE, YOU!
?
!

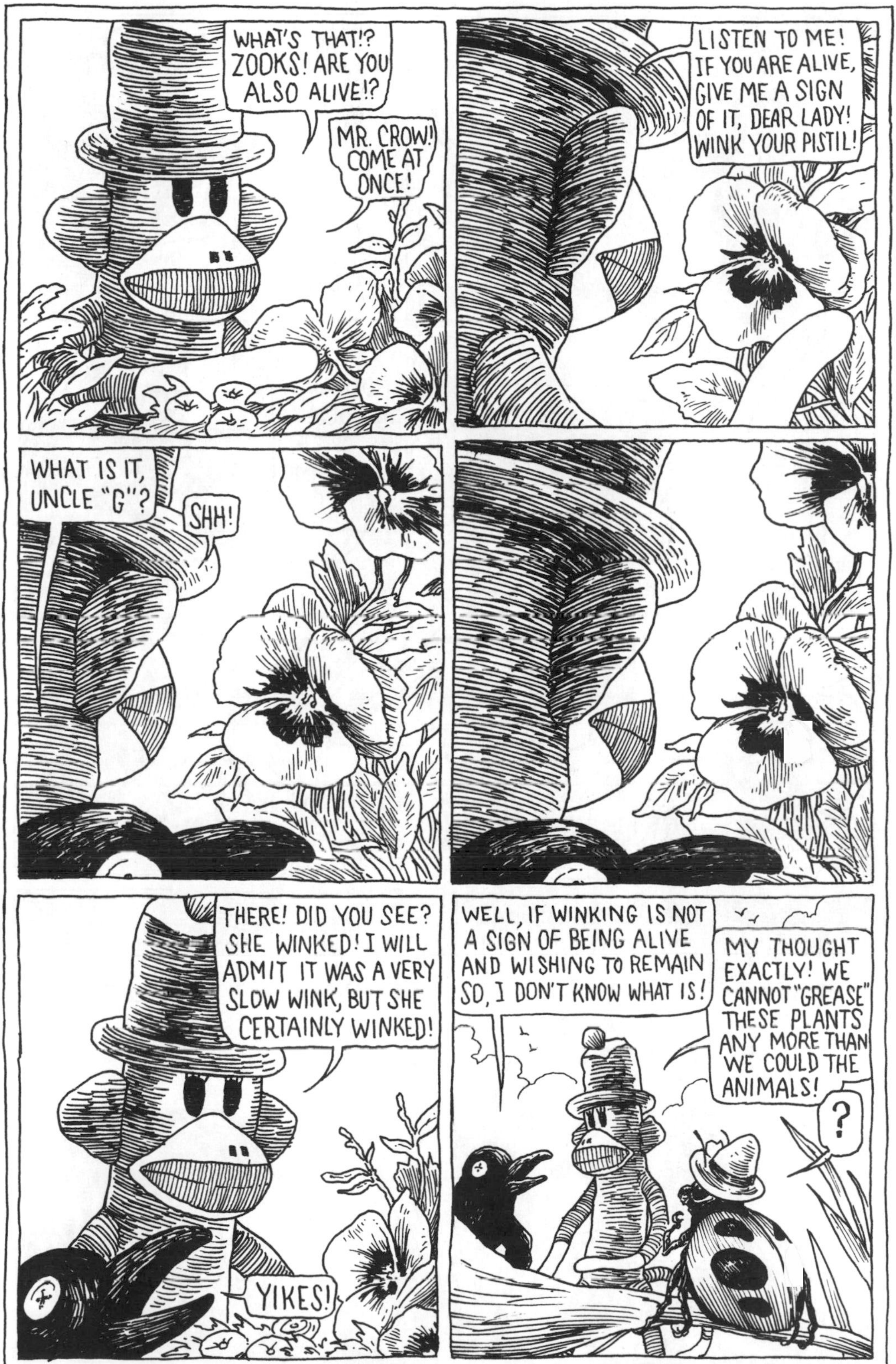
WHAT'S THAT!? ZOOKS! ARE YOU ALSO ALIVE!?
MR. CROW! COME AT ONCE!
LISTEN TO ME! IF YOU ARE ALIVE, GIVE ME A SIGN OF IT, DEAR LADY! WINK YOUR PISTIL!
WHAT IS IT, UNCLE "G"?
SHH!
THERE! DID YOU SEE? SHE WINKED! I WILL ADMIT IT WAS A VERY SLOW WINK, BUT SHE CERTAINLY WINKED!
YIKES!
WELL, IF WINKING IS NOT A SIGN OF BEING ALIVE AND WISHING TO REMAIN SO, I DON'T KNOW WHAT IS!
MY THOUGHT EXACTLY! WE CANNOT "GREASE" THESE PLANTS ANY MORE THAN WE COULD THE ANIMALS!
?

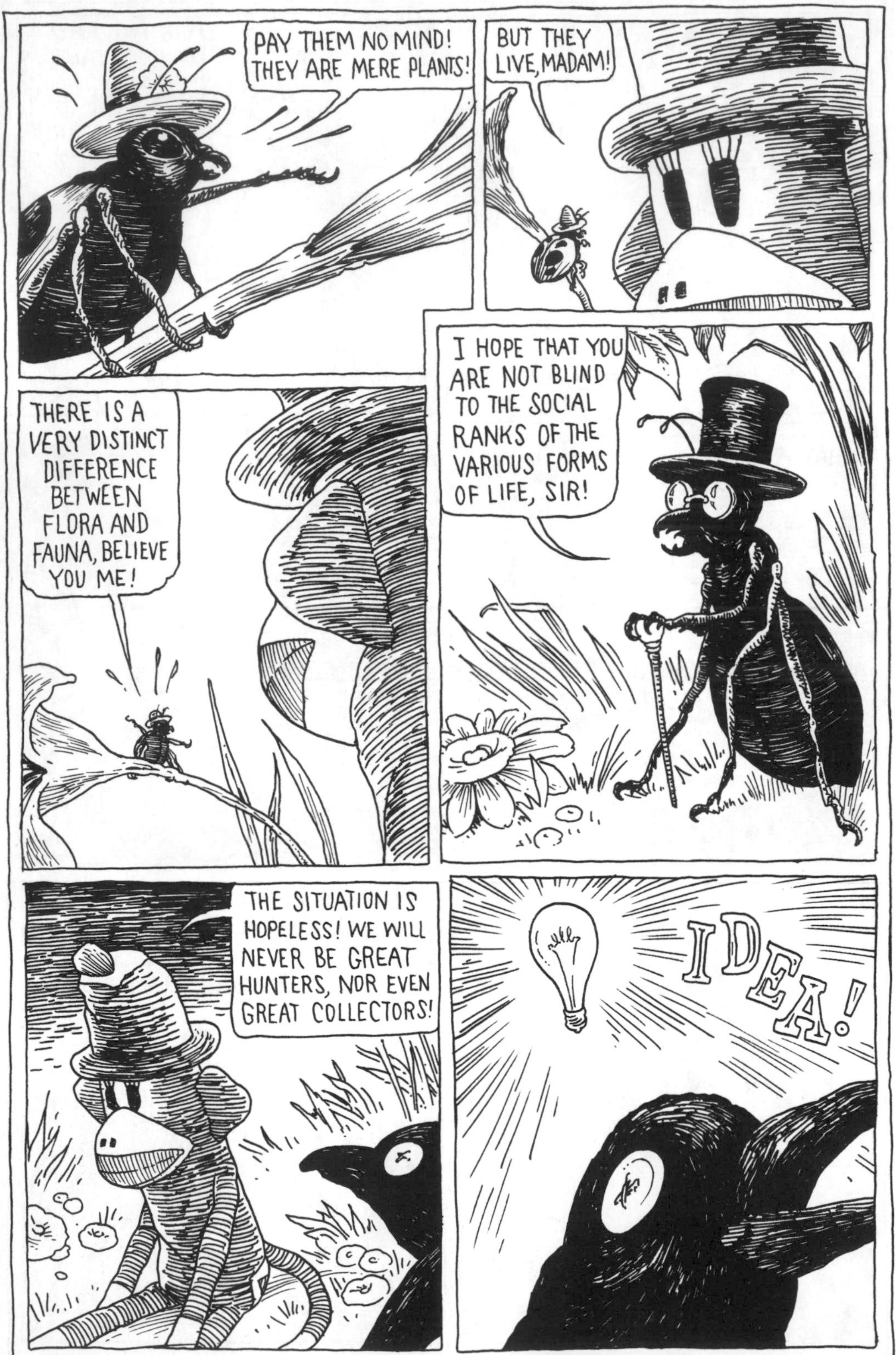
PAY THEM NO MIND! THEY ARE MERE PLANTS!
BUT THEY LIVE, MADAM!
THERE IS A VERY DISTINCT DIFFERENCE BETWEEN FLORA AND FAUNA, BELIEVE YOU ME!
I HOPE THAT YOU ARE NOT BLIND TO THE SOCIAL RANKS OF THE VARIOUS FORMS OF LIFE, SIR!
THE SITUATION IS HOPELESS! WE WILL NEVER BE GREAT HUNTERS, NOR EVEN GREAT COLLECTORS!
IDEA!

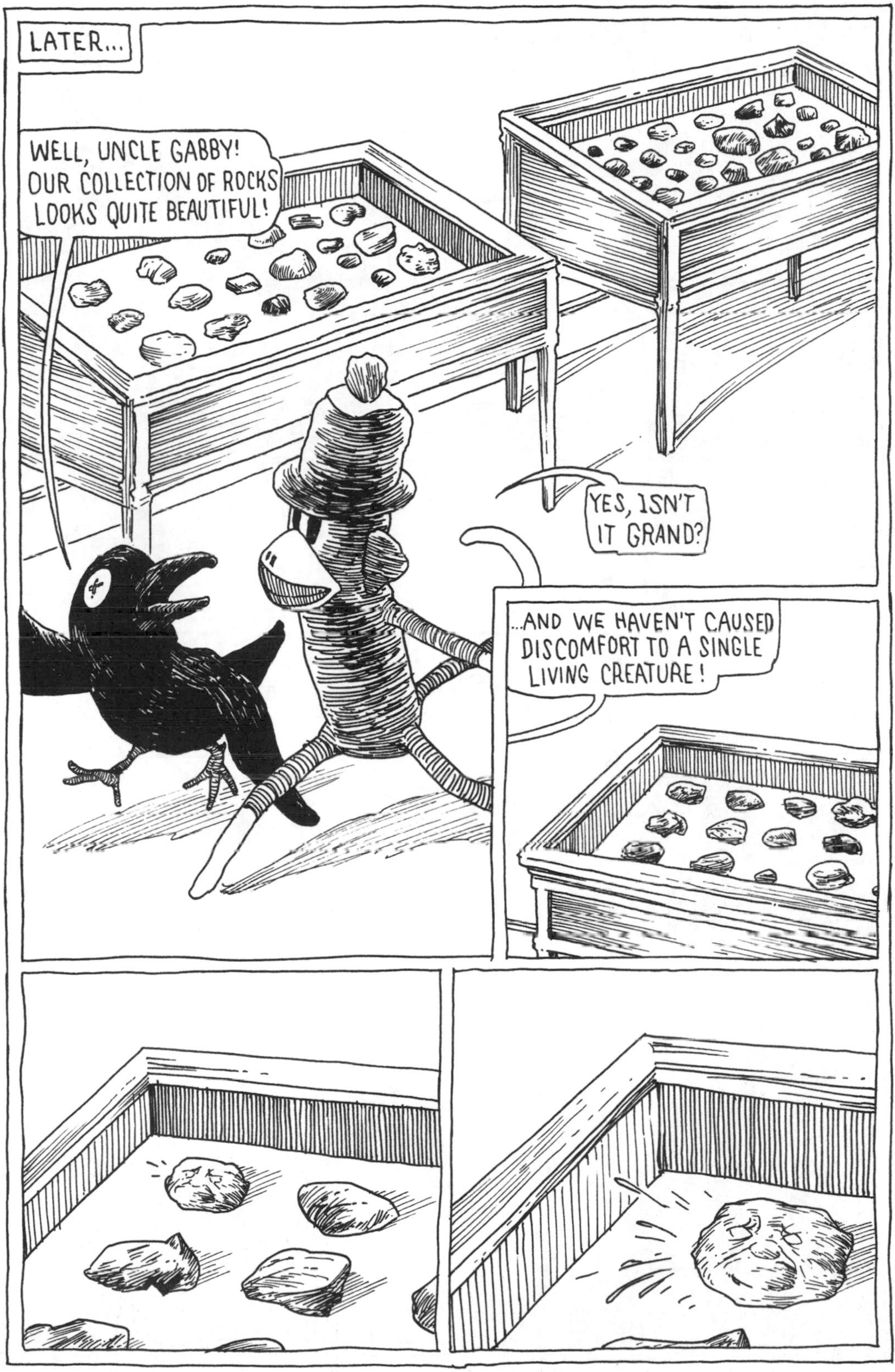
LATER...
WELL, UNCLE GABBY! OUR COLLECTION OF ROCKS LOOKS QUITE BEAUTIFUL!
YES, ISN'T IT GRAND?
...AND WE HAVEN'T CAUSED DISCOMFORT TO A SINGLE LIVING CREATURE!

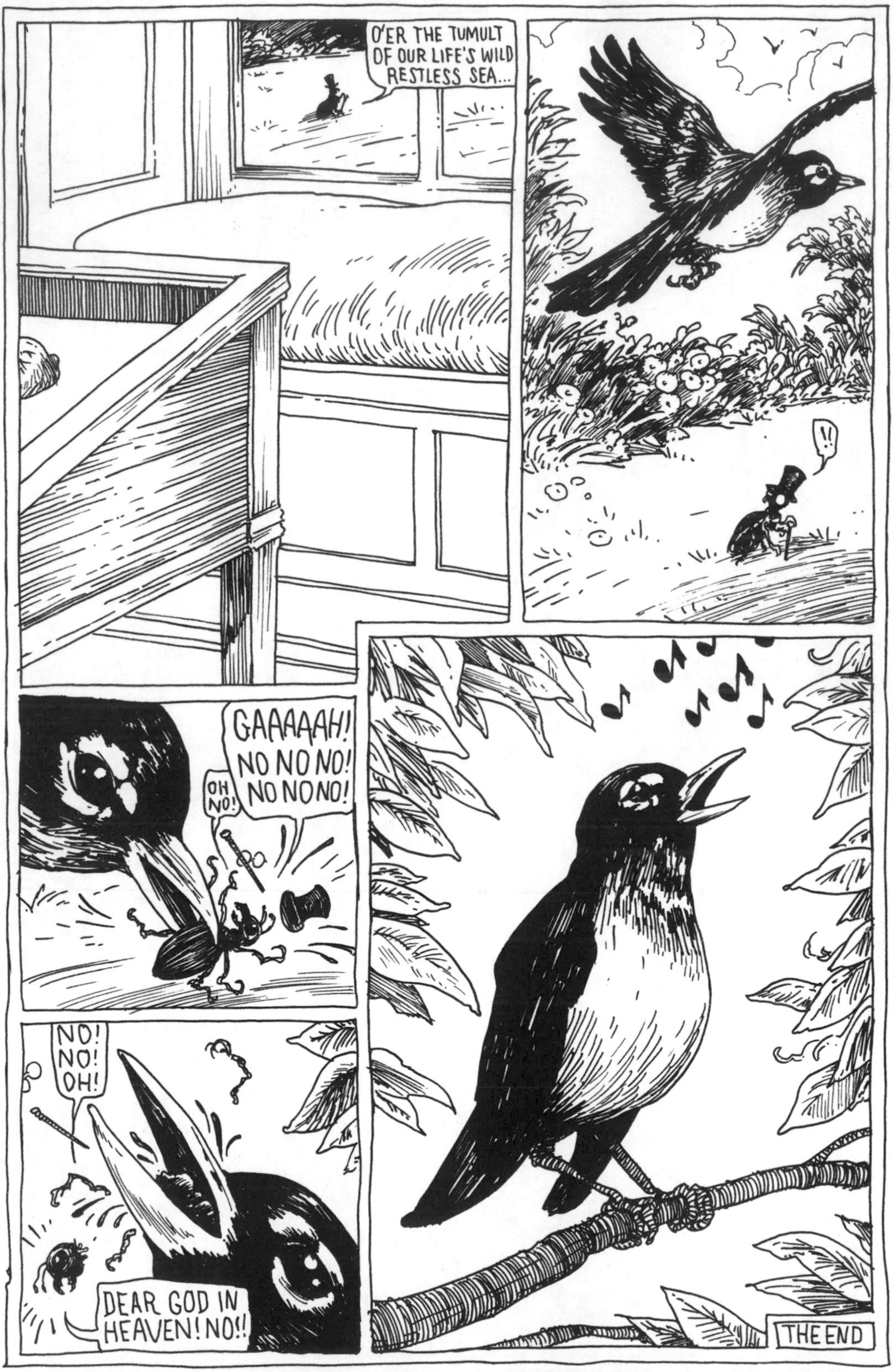
O'ER THE TUMULT OF OUR LIFE'S WILD RESTLESS SEA...
!!
GAAAAAH! NO NO NO! NO NO NO!
OH NO!
NO! NO! OH!
DEAR GOD IN HEAVEN! NO!!
THE END

# PROFILE OF A HERO

By Tony Millionaire

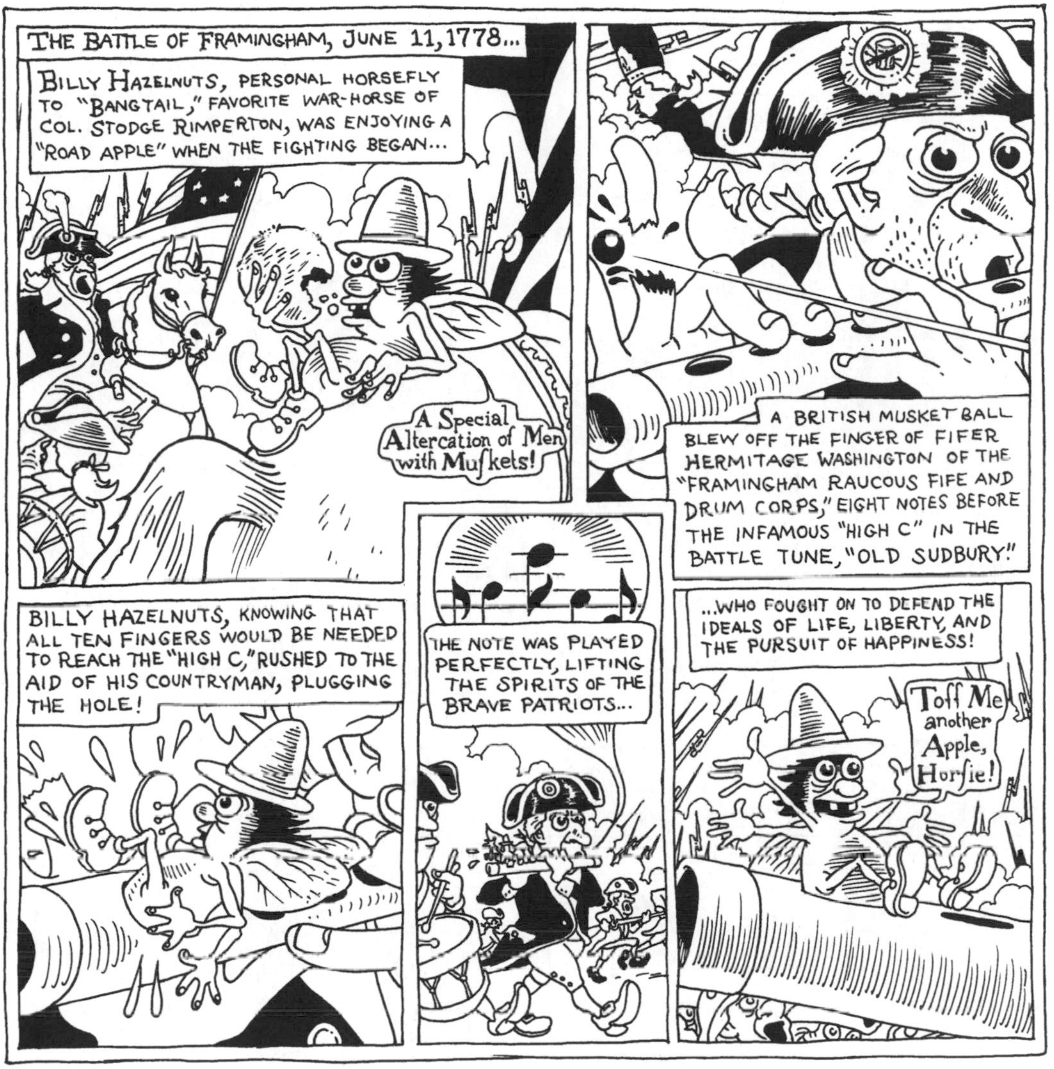

THE BATTLE OF FRAMINGHAM, JUNE 11, 1778...
BILLY HAZELNUTS, PERSONAL HORSEFLY TO "BANGTAIL," FAVORITE WAR-HORSE OF COL. STODGE RIMPERTON, WAS ENJOYING A "ROAD APPLE" WHEN THE FIGHTING BEGAN...
A Special Altercation of Men with Muſkets!
A BRITISH MUSKET BALL BLEW OFF THE FINGER OF FIFER HERMITAGE WASHINGTON OF THE "FRAMINGHAM RAUCOUS FIFE AND DRUM CORPS," EIGHT NOTES BEFORE THE INFAMOUS "HIGH C" IN THE BATTLE TUNE, "OLD SUDBURY."
BILLY HAZELNUTS, KNOWING THAT ALL TEN FINGERS WOULD BE NEEDED TO REACH THE "HIGH C," RUSHED TO THE AID OF HIS COUNTRYMAN, PLUGGING THE HOLE!
THE NOTE WAS PLAYED PERFECTLY, LIFTING THE SPIRITS OF THE BRAVE PATRIOTS...
...WHO FOUGHT ON TO DEFEND THE IDEALS OF LIFE, LIBERTY, AND THE PURSUIT OF HAPPINESS!
Toſſ Me another Apple, Horſie!


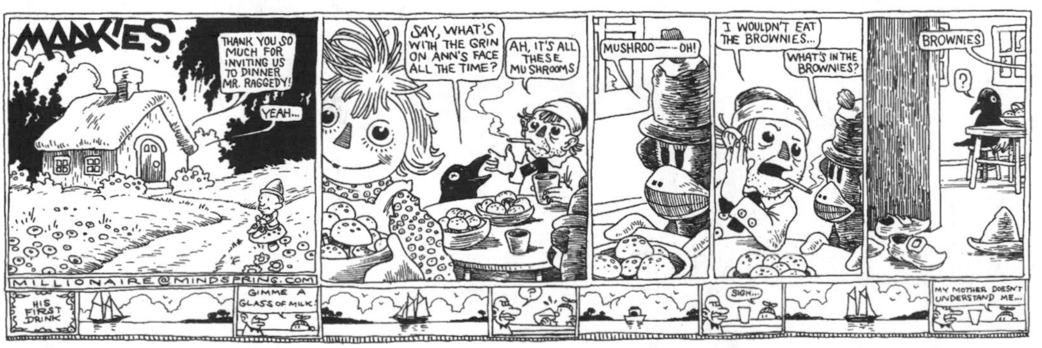

MAAKIES
THANK YOU SO MUCH FOR INVITING US TO DINNER MR. RAGGEDY!
YEAH...
SAY, WHAT'S WITH THE GRIN ON ANN'S FACE ALL THE TIME?
AH, IT'S ALL THESE MUSHROOMS
MUSHROO——OH!
I WOULDN'T EAT THE BROWNIES...
WHAT'S IN THE BROWNIES?
BROWNIES
?
MILLIONAIRE@MINDSPRING.COM
HIS FIRST DRINK
GIMME A GLASS OF MILK!
?
SIGH...
MY MOTHER DOESN'T UNDERSTAND ME...

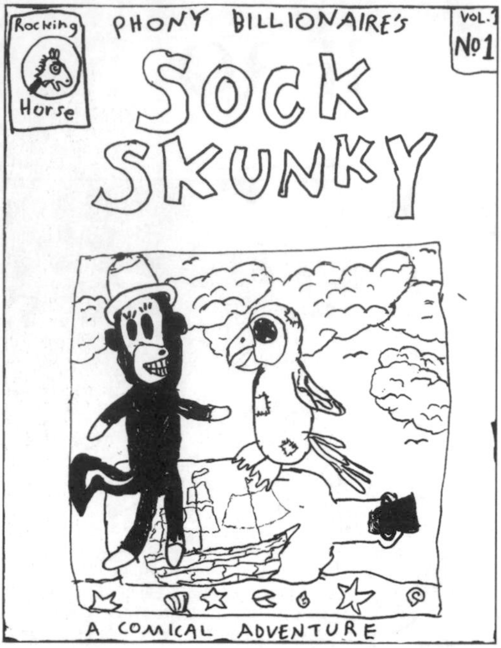
Rocking Horse
PHONY BILLIONAIRE'S
VOL. 1 No 1
SOCK SKUNKY
A COMICAL ADVENTURE

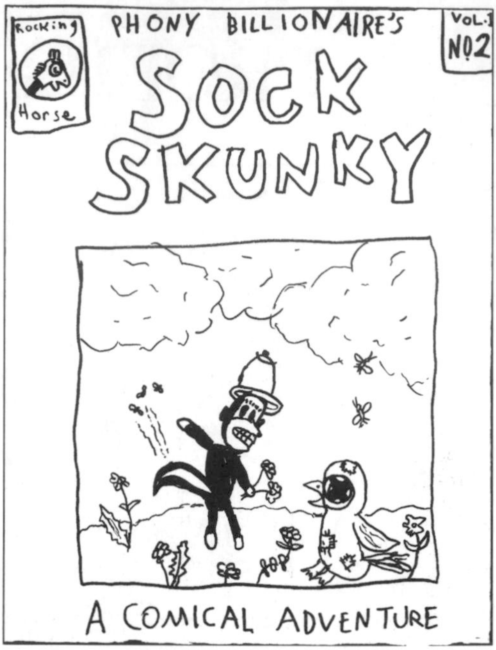
Rocking Horse
PHONY BILLIONAIRE'S
VOL. 1 No 2
SOCK SKUNKY
A COMICAL ADVENTURE

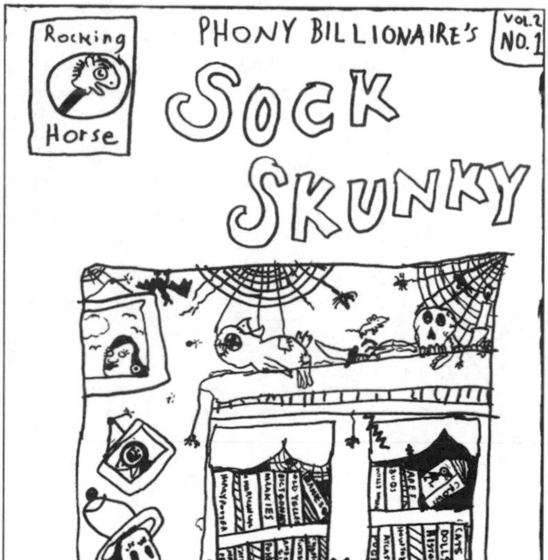
Rocking Horse
PHONY BILLIONAIRE'S
VOL. 2 NO. 1
SOCK SKUNKY
A COMICAL ADVENTURE

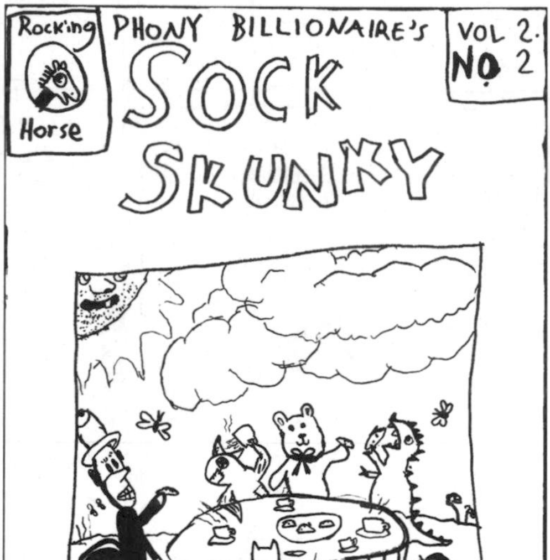
Rocking Horse
PHONY BILLIONAIRE'S
VOL 2. NO 2
SOCK SKUNKY
A COMICAL ADVENTURE

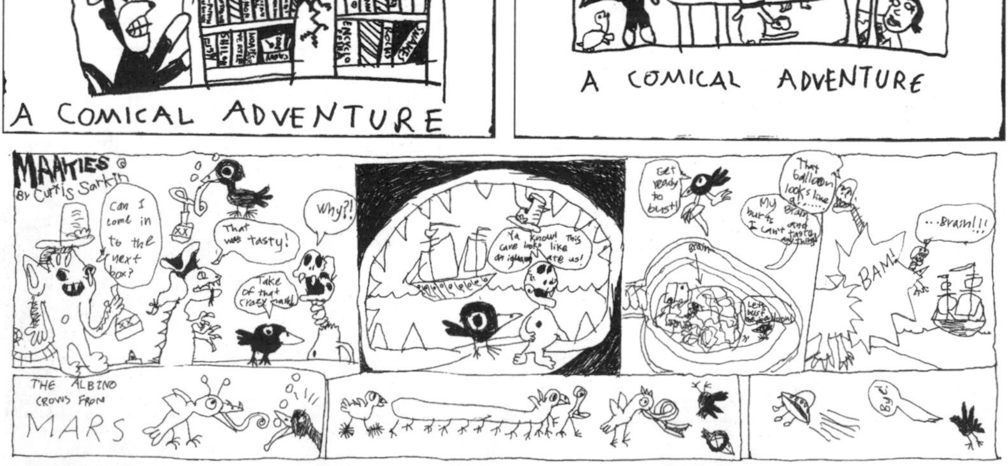
MAAKIES ©
By Curtis Sarkin
Can I come in to the next box?
That was tasty!
Why?!
Ya know! This cave looks like an iglo
ate us!
Get ready to bust!
That balloon looks like a......
My Brain hurts and I can't taste anything!
Brain
BAM!
...Brain!!!
THE ALBINO CROWS FROM MARS
Bye!

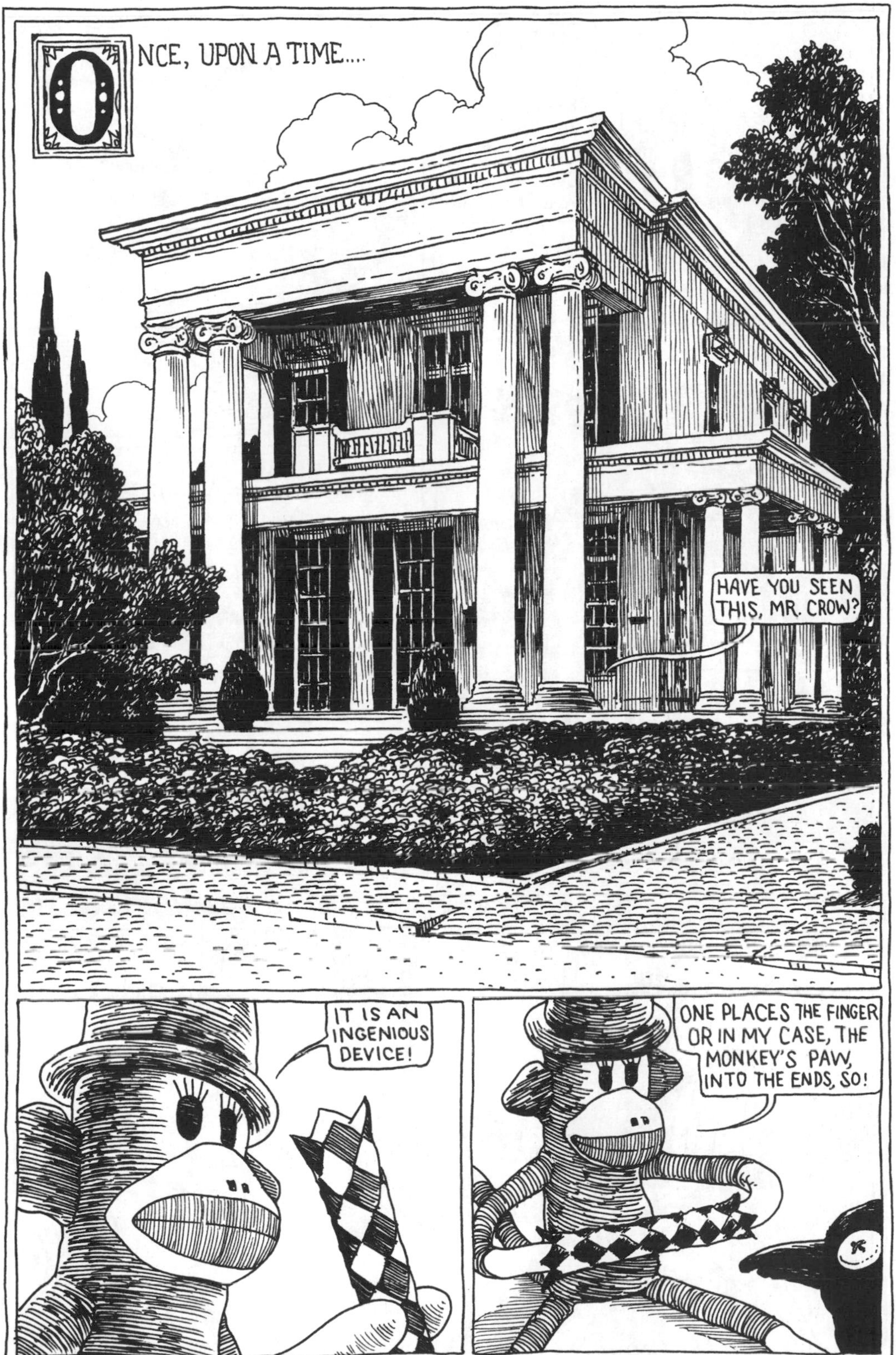
ONCE, UPON A TIME....
HAVE YOU SEEN THIS, MR. CROW?
IT IS AN INGENIOUS DEVICE!
ONE PLACES THE FINGER OR IN MY CASE, THE MONKEY'S PAW, INTO THE ENDS, SO!

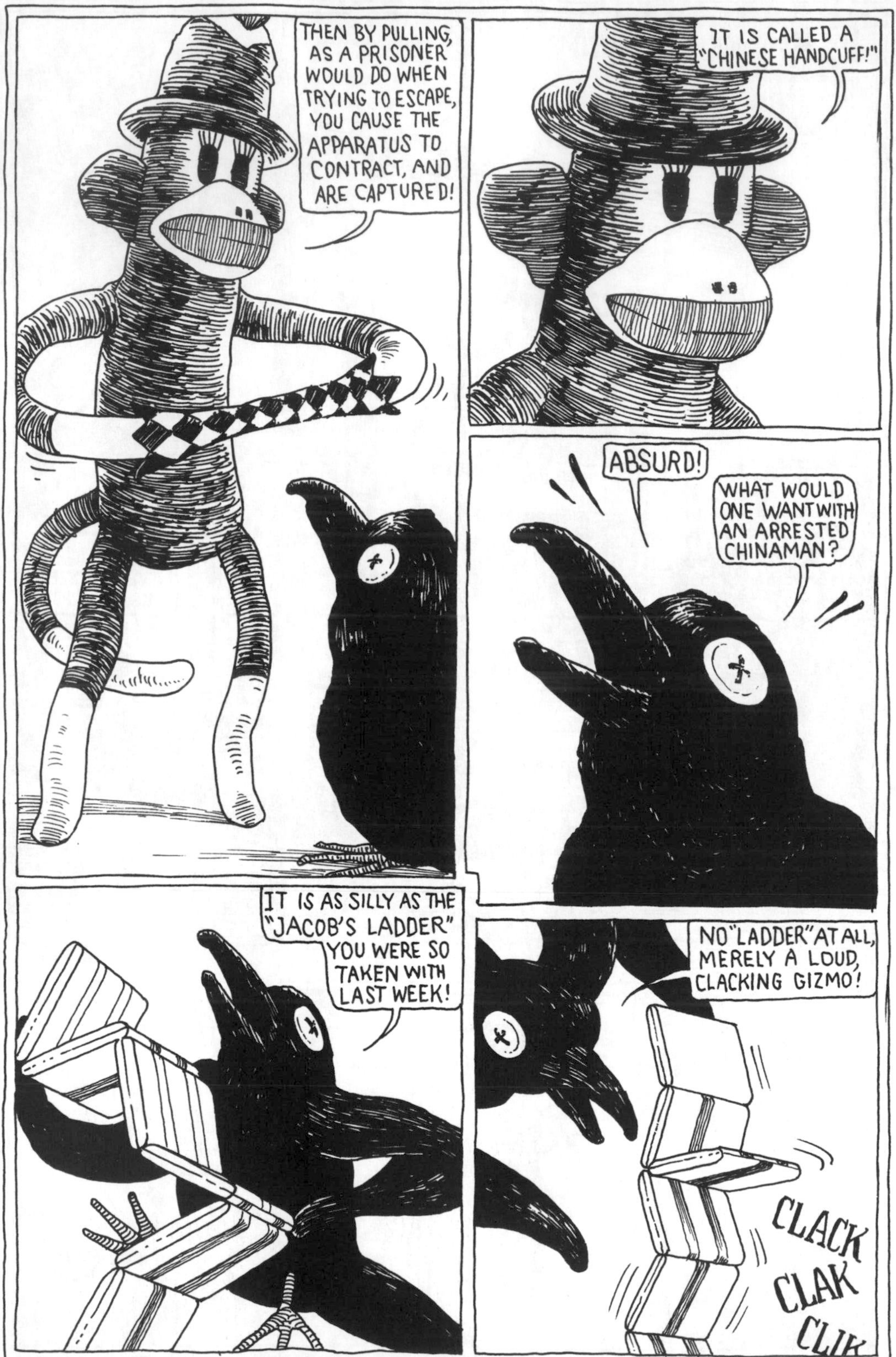
THEN BY PULLING, AS A PRISONER WOULD DO WHEN TRYING TO ESCAPE, YOU CAUSE THE APPARATUS TO CONTRACT, AND ARE CAPTURED!
IT IS CALLED A "CHINESE HANDCUFF!"
ABSURD!
WHAT WOULD ONE WANT WITH AN ARRESTED CHINAMAN?
IT IS AS SILLY AS THE "JACOB'S LADDER" YOU WERE SO TAKEN WITH LAST WEEK!
NO "LADDER" AT ALL, MERELY A LOUD, CLACKING GIZMO!
CLACK
CLAK
CLIK

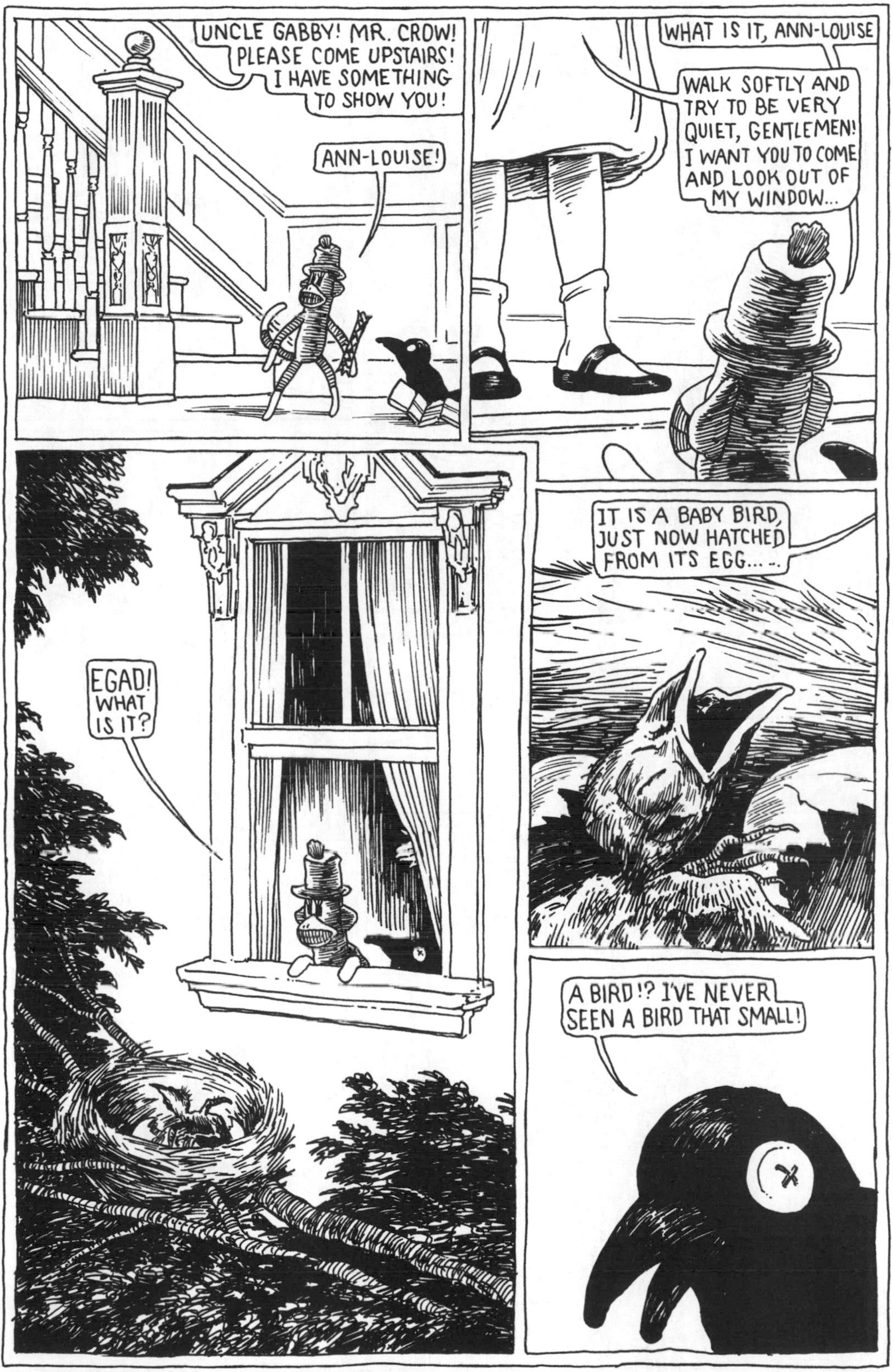
UNCLE GABBY! MR. CROW! PLEASE COME UPSTAIRS! I HAVE SOMETHING TO SHOW YOU!
ANN-LOUISE!
WHAT IS IT, ANN-LOUISE
WALK SOFTLY AND TRY TO BE VERY QUIET, GENTLEMEN! I WANT YOU TO COME AND LOOK OUT OF MY WINDOW...
EGAD! WHAT IS IT?
IT IS A BABY BIRD, JUST NOW HATCHED FROM ITS EGG....
A BIRD!? I'VE NEVER SEEN A BIRD THAT SMALL!

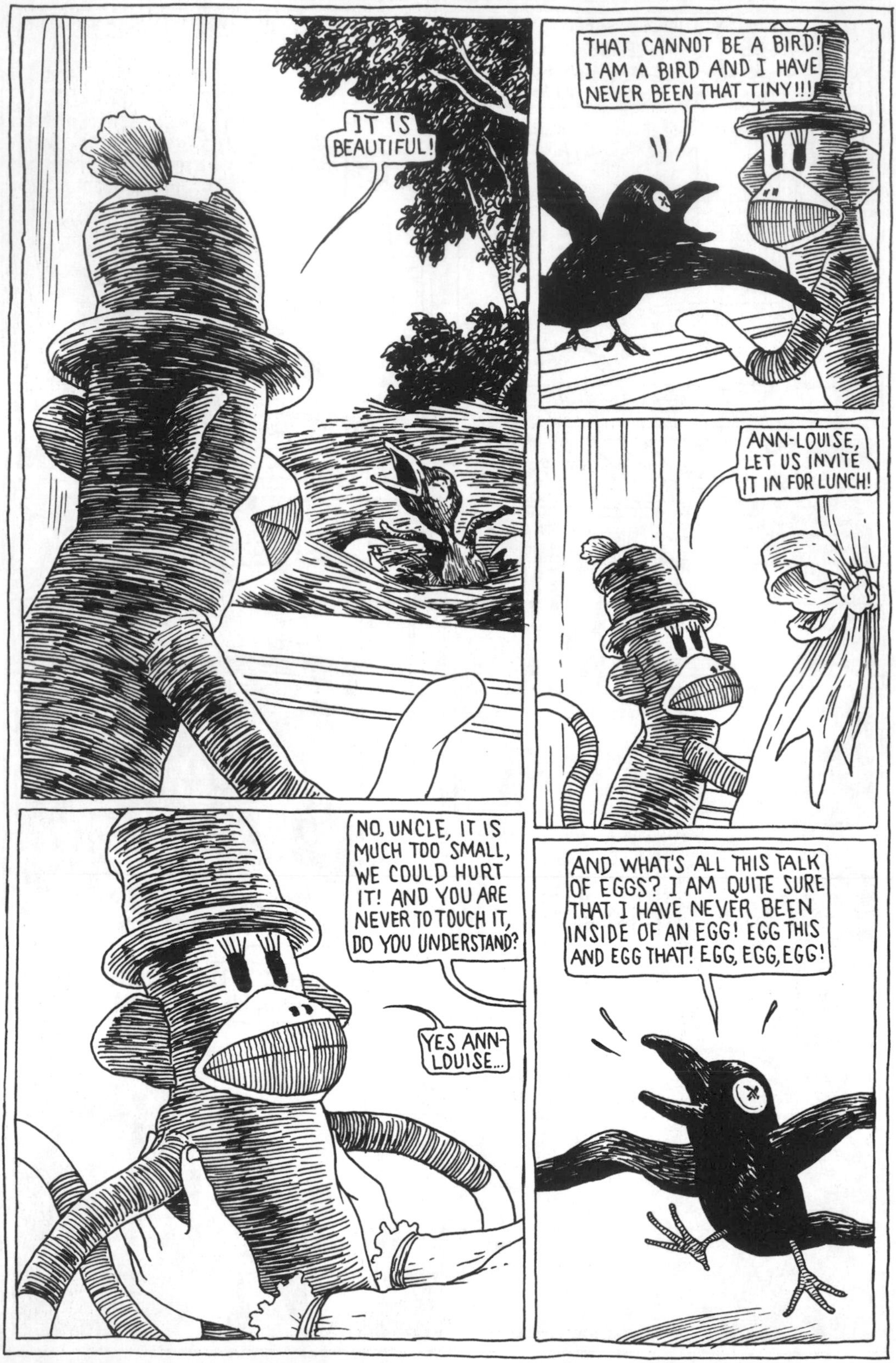
IT IS BEAUTIFUL!
THAT CANNOT BE A BIRD! I AM A BIRD AND I HAVE NEVER BEEN THAT TINY!!!
ANN-LOUISE, LET US INVITE IT IN FOR LUNCH!
NO, UNCLE, IT IS MUCH TOO SMALL, WE COULD HURT IT! AND YOU ARE NEVER TO TOUCH IT, DO YOU UNDERSTAND?
YES ANN-LOUISE...
AND WHAT'S ALL THIS TALK OF EGGS? I AM QUITE SURE THAT I HAVE NEVER BEEN INSIDE OF AN EGG! EGG THIS AND EGG THAT! EGG, EGG, EGG!

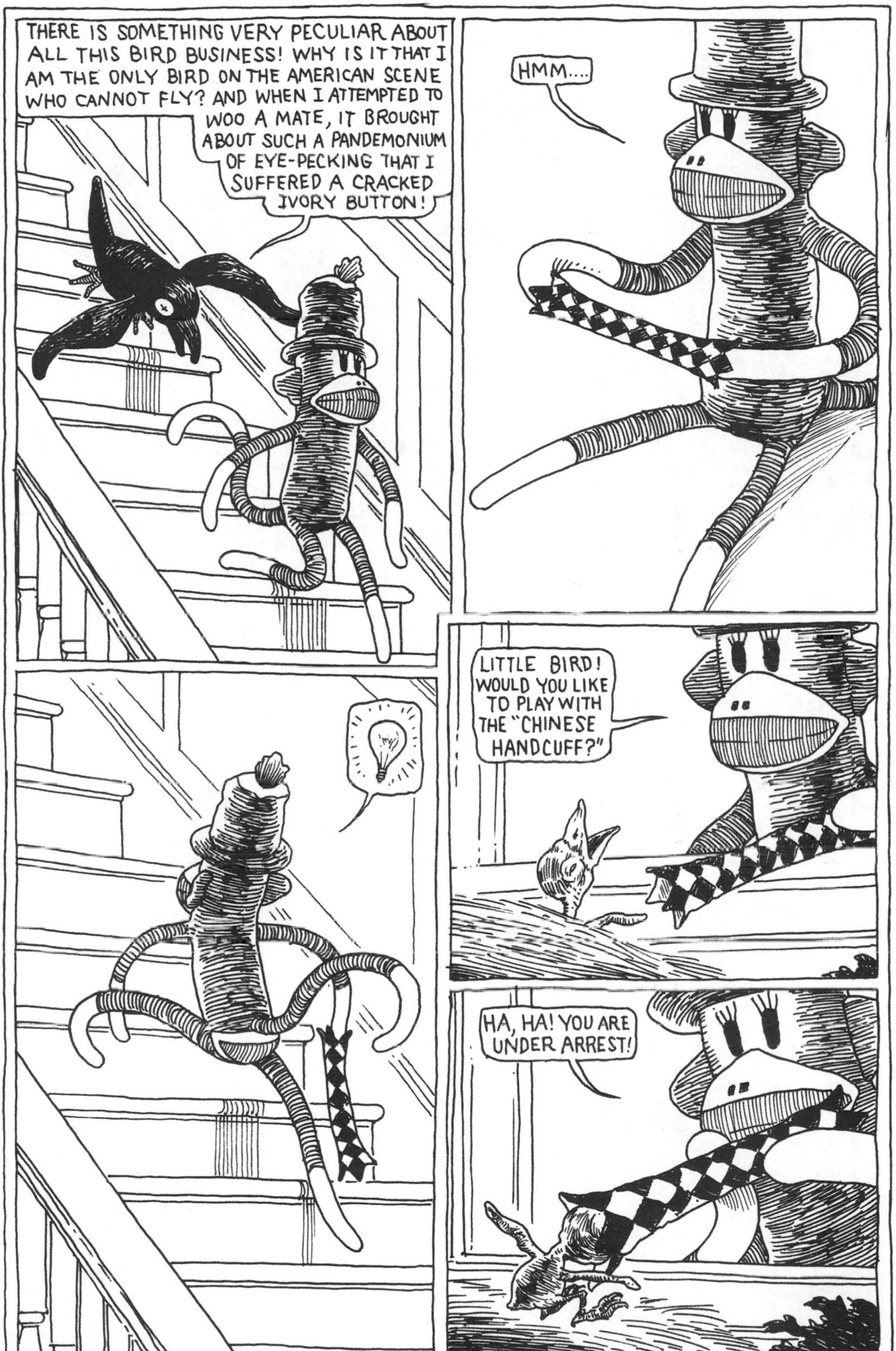
THERE IS SOMETHING VERY PECULIAR ABOUT ALL THIS BIRD BUSINESS! WHY IS IT THAT I AM THE ONLY BIRD ON THE AMERICAN SCENE WHO CANNOT FLY? AND WHEN I ATTEMPTED TO WOO A MATE, IT BROUGHT ABOUT SUCH A PANDEMONIUM OF EYE-PECKING THAT I SUFFERED A CRACKED IVORY BUTTON!
HMM....
LITTLE BIRD! WOULD YOU LIKE TO PLAY WITH THE "CHINESE HANDCUFF?"
HA, HA! YOU ARE UNDER ARREST!

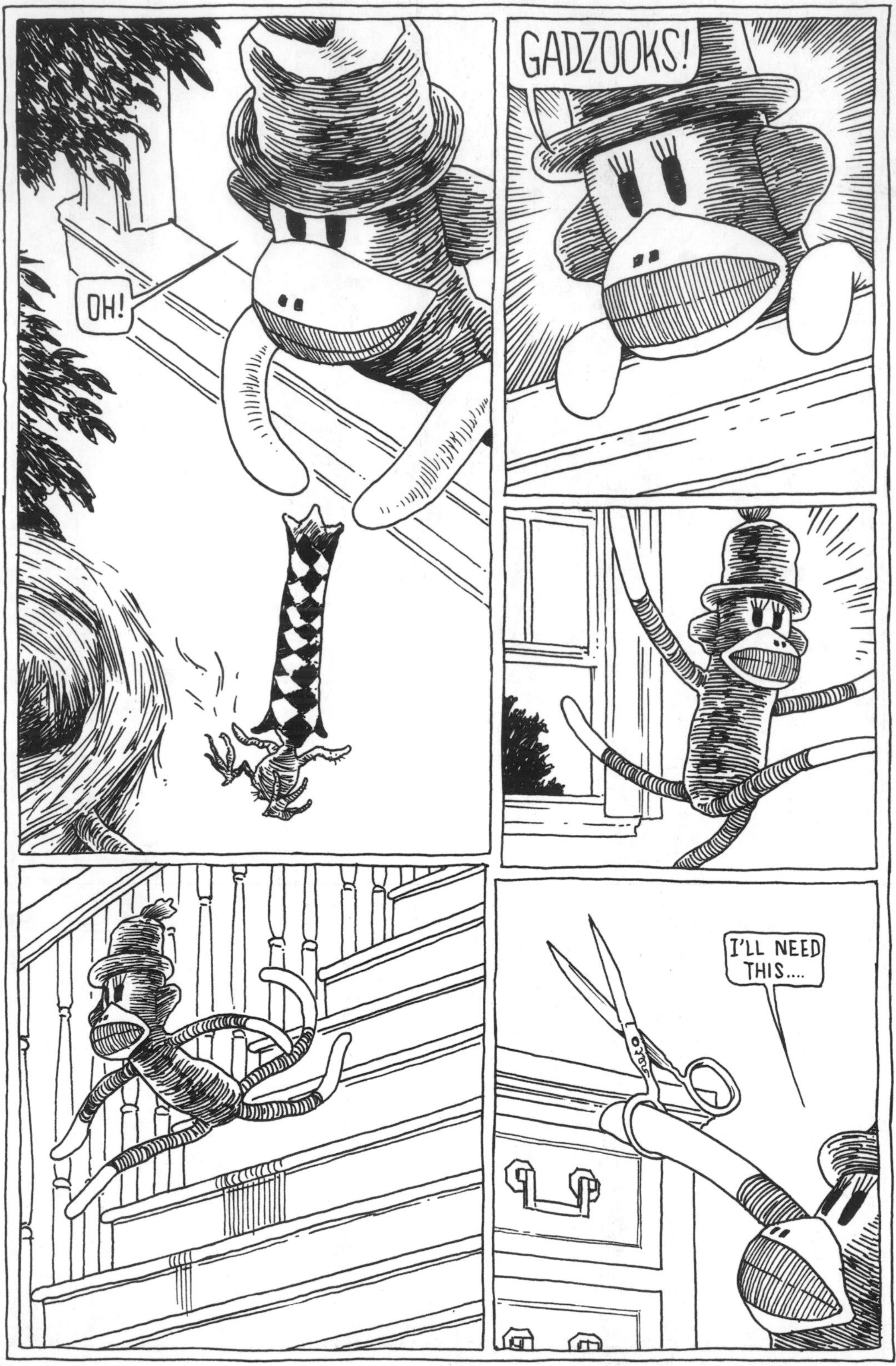
OH!
GADZOOKS!
I'LL NEED THIS....

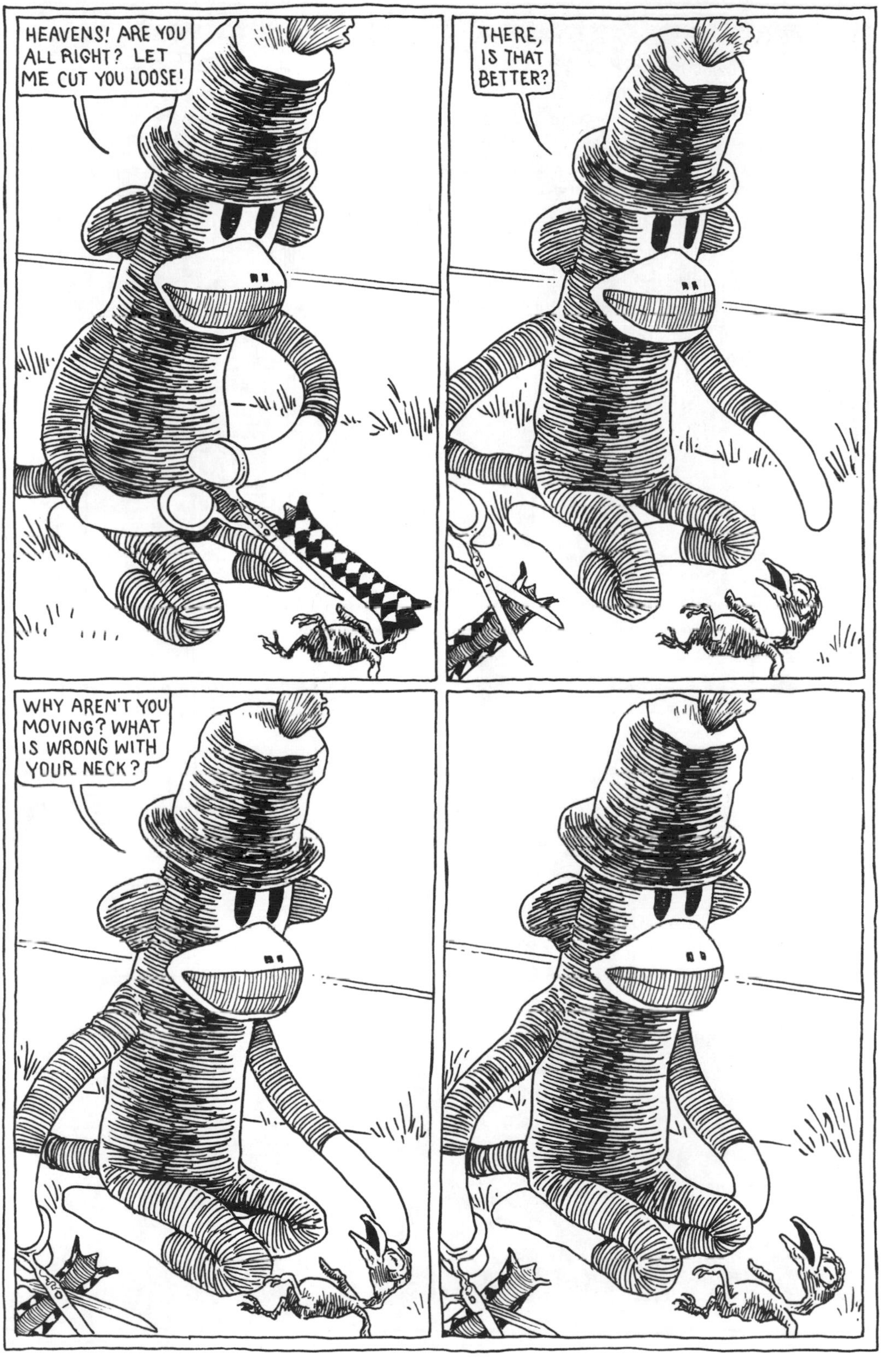
HEAVENS! ARE YOU ALL RIGHT? LET ME CUT YOU LOOSE!
THERE, IS THAT BETTER?
WHY AREN'T YOU MOVING? WHAT IS WRONG WITH YOUR NECK?

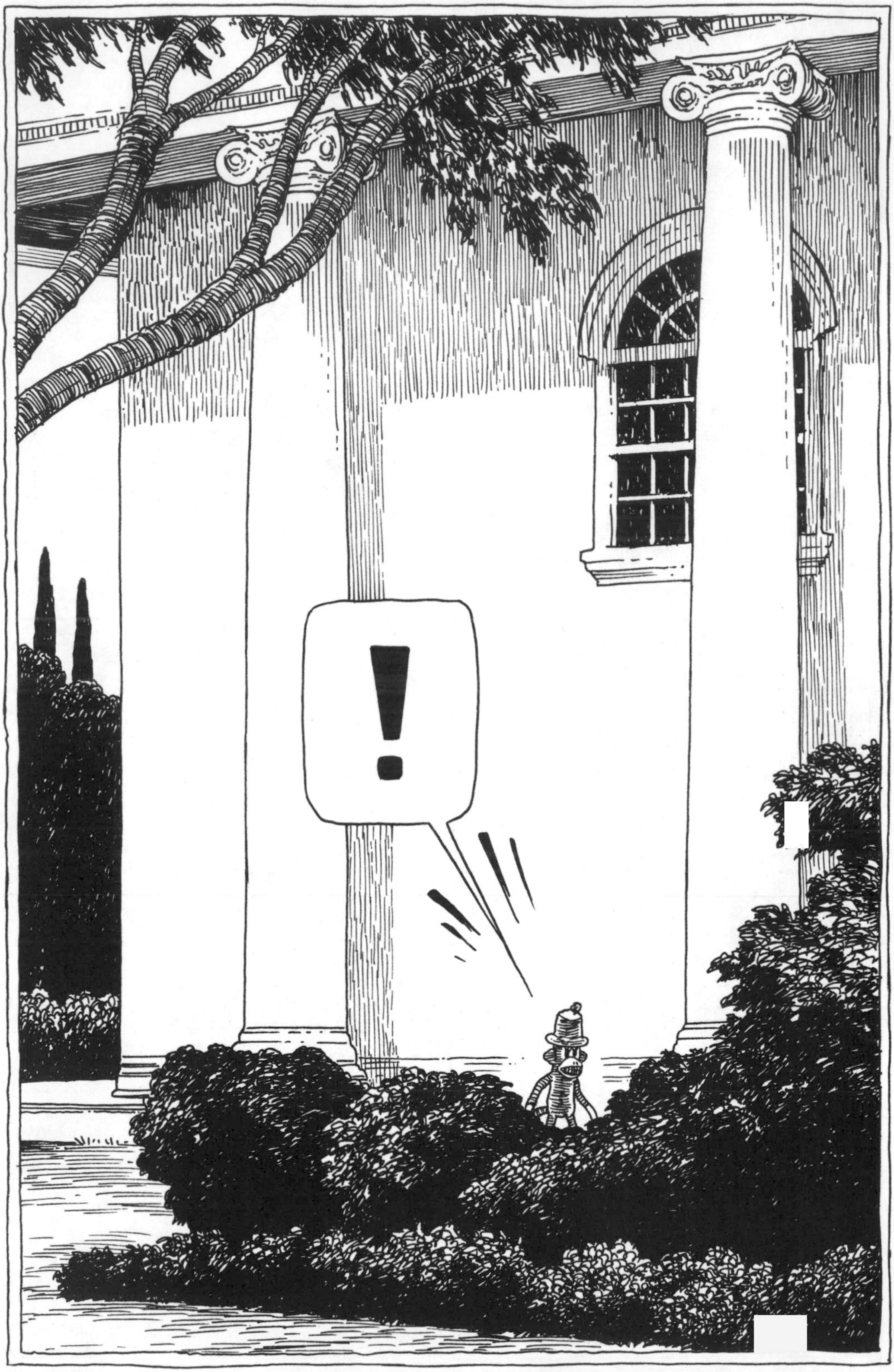
!

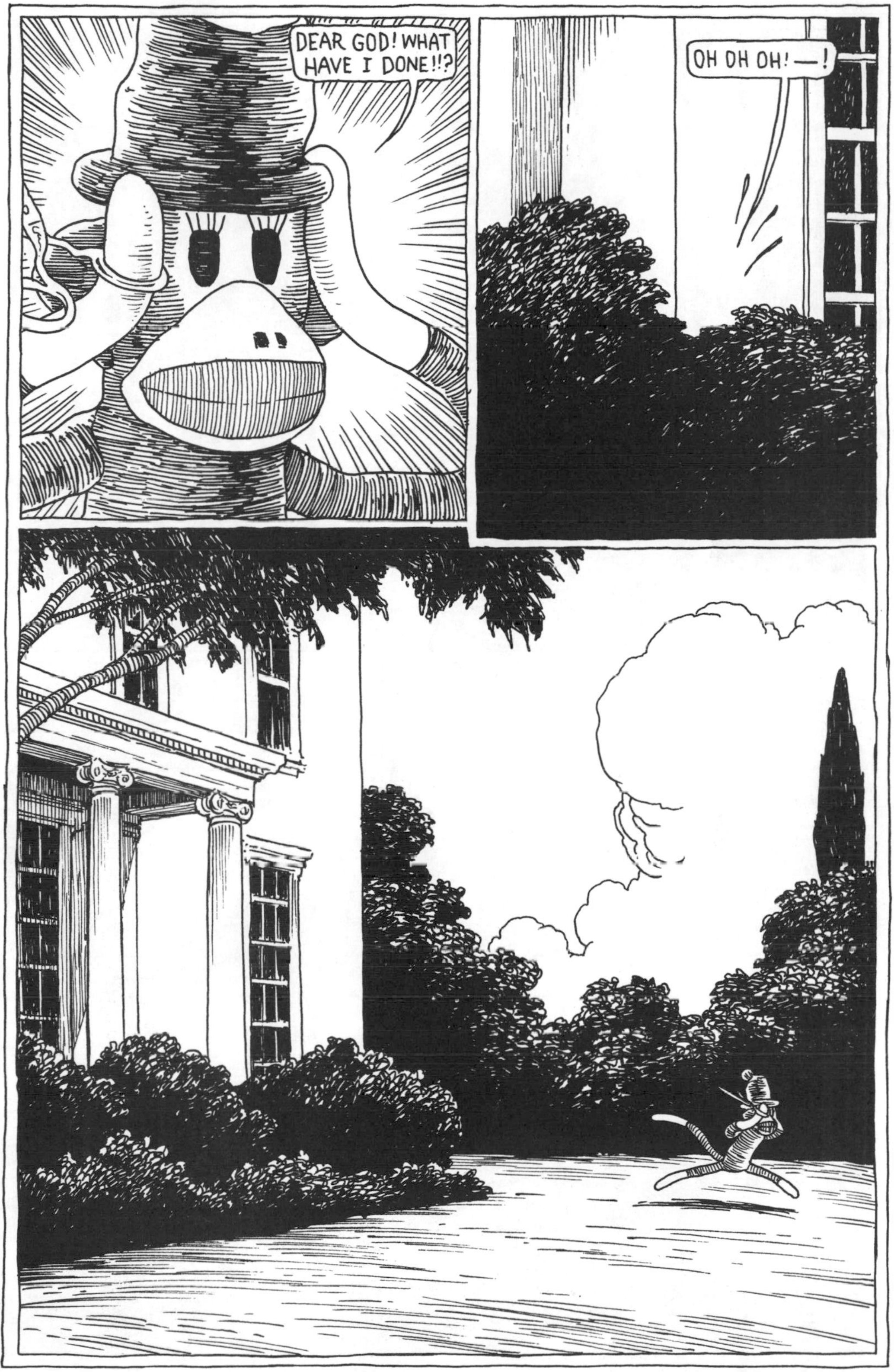
DEAR GOD! WHAT HAVE I DONE!!?
OH OH OH! —!

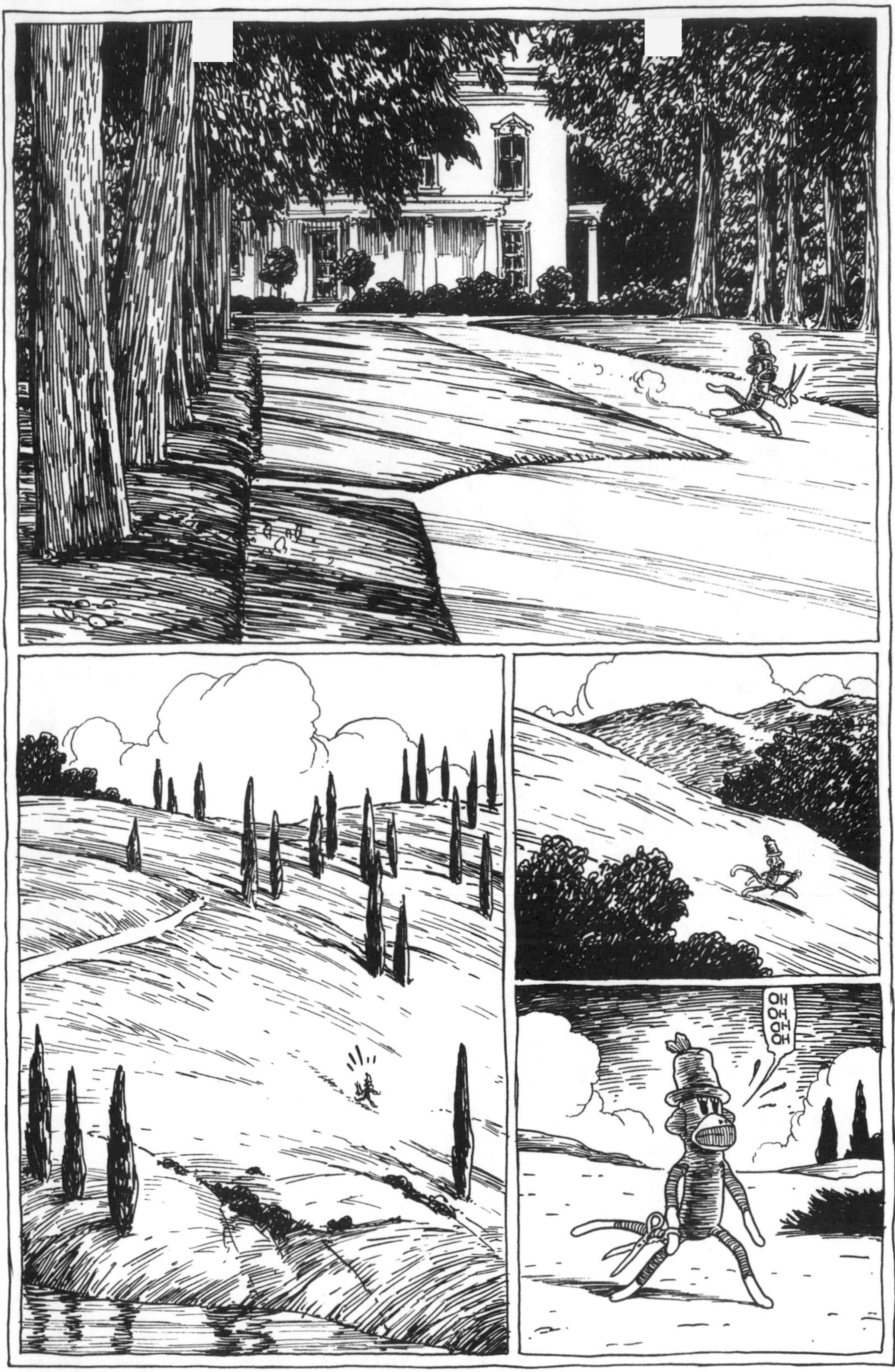
OH OH OH OH

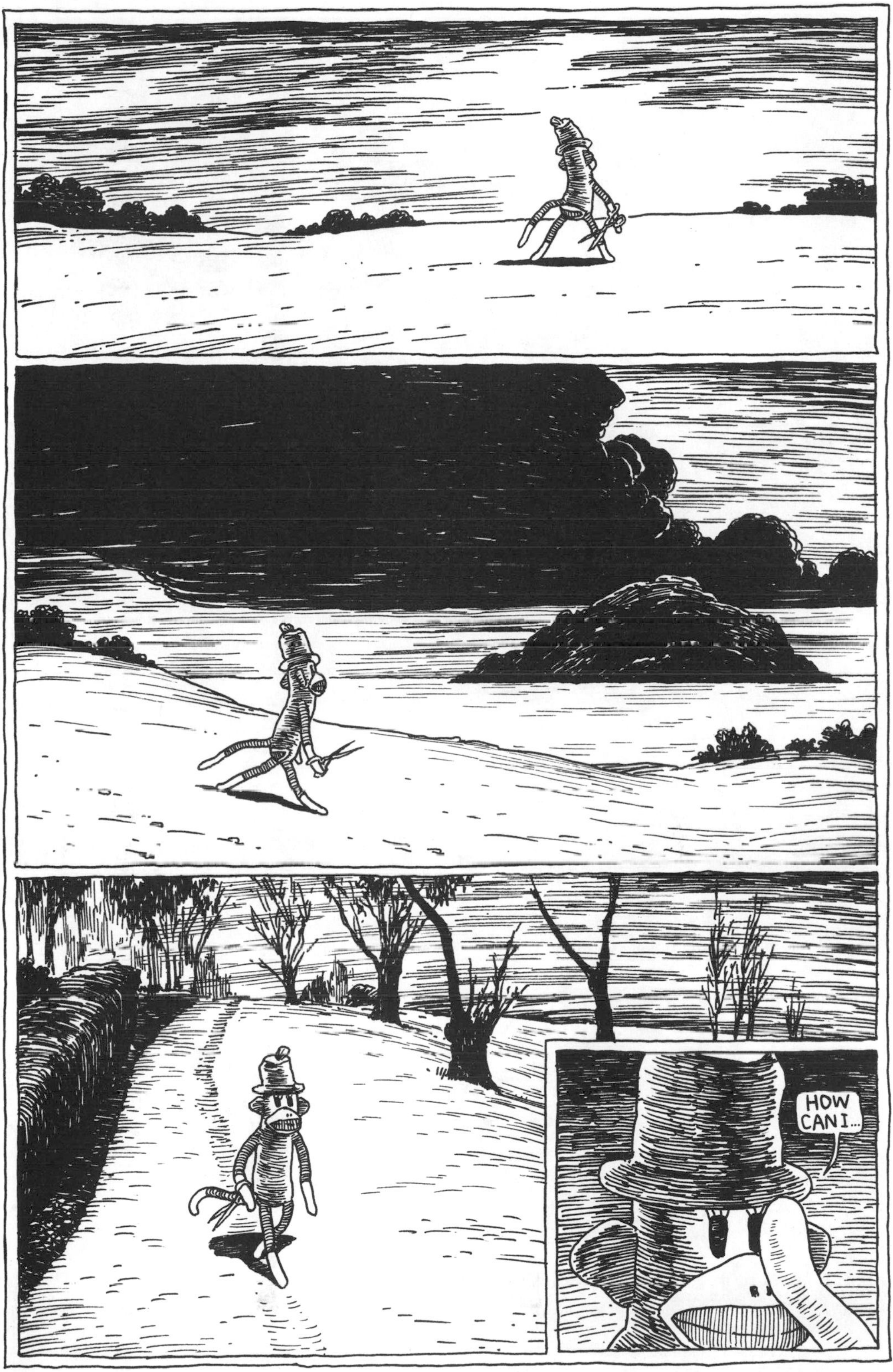
HOW CAN I...

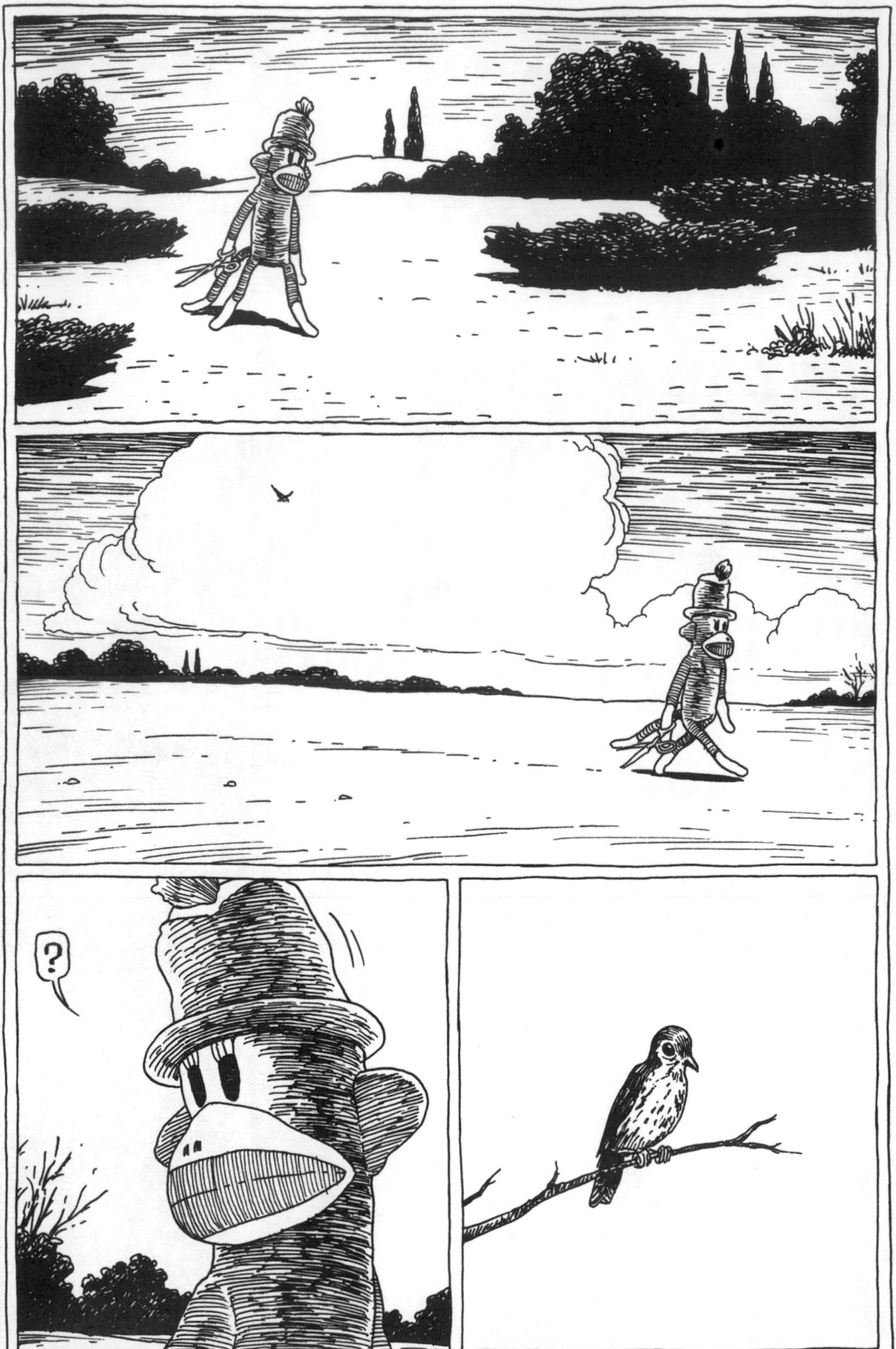
?

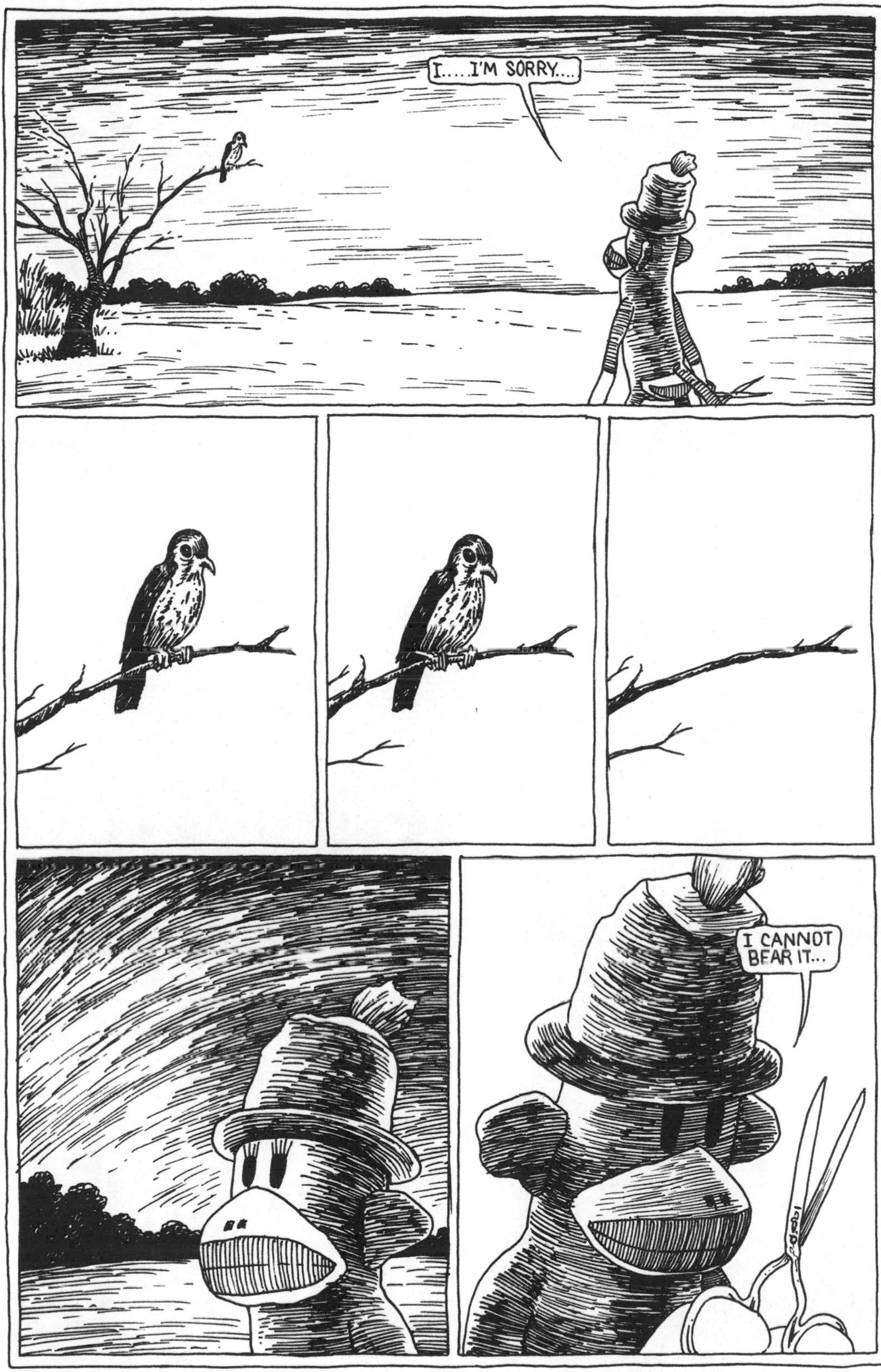
I.....I'M SORRY....
I CANNOT BEAR IT...

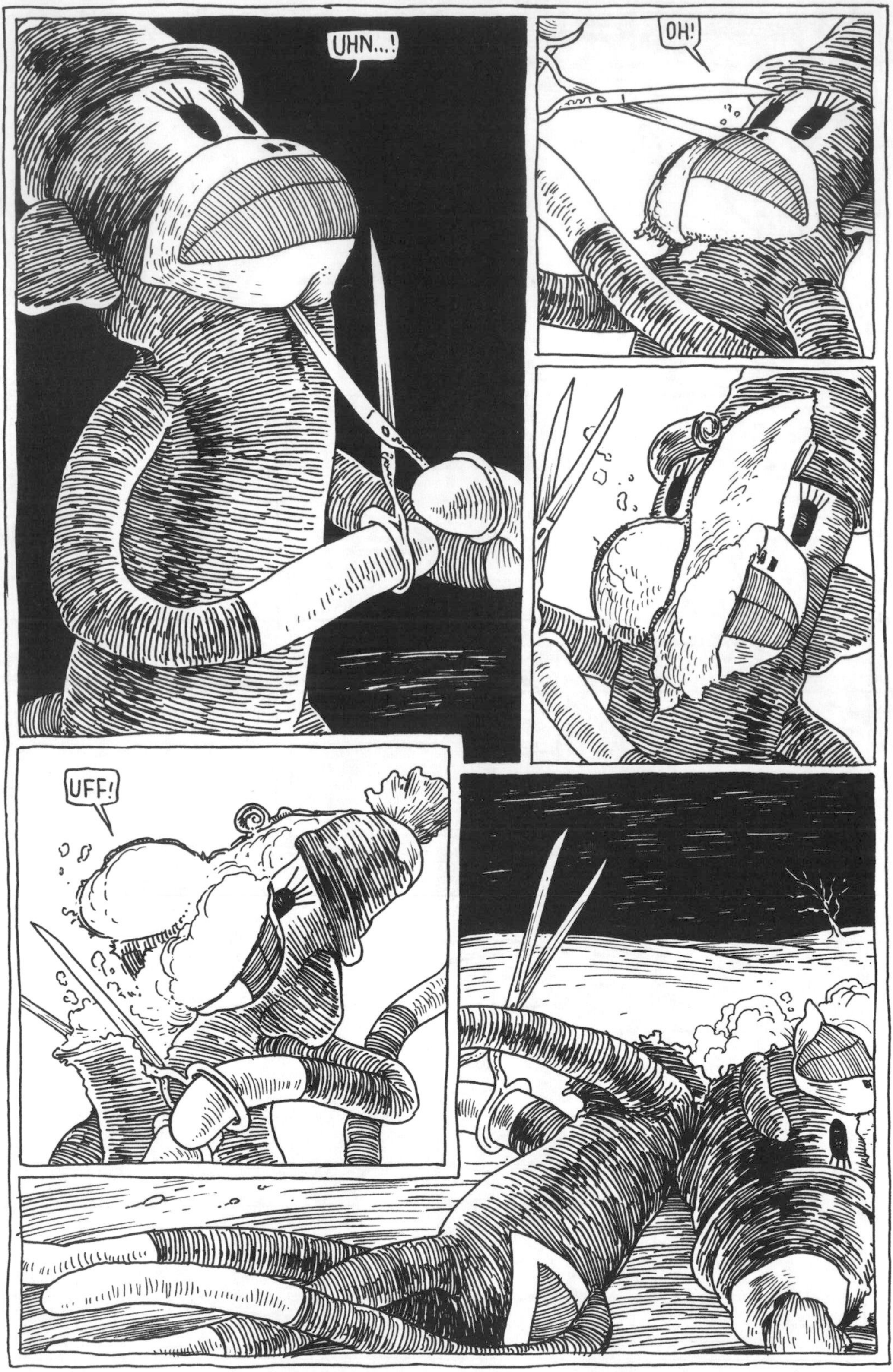
UHN...!
OH!
UFF!

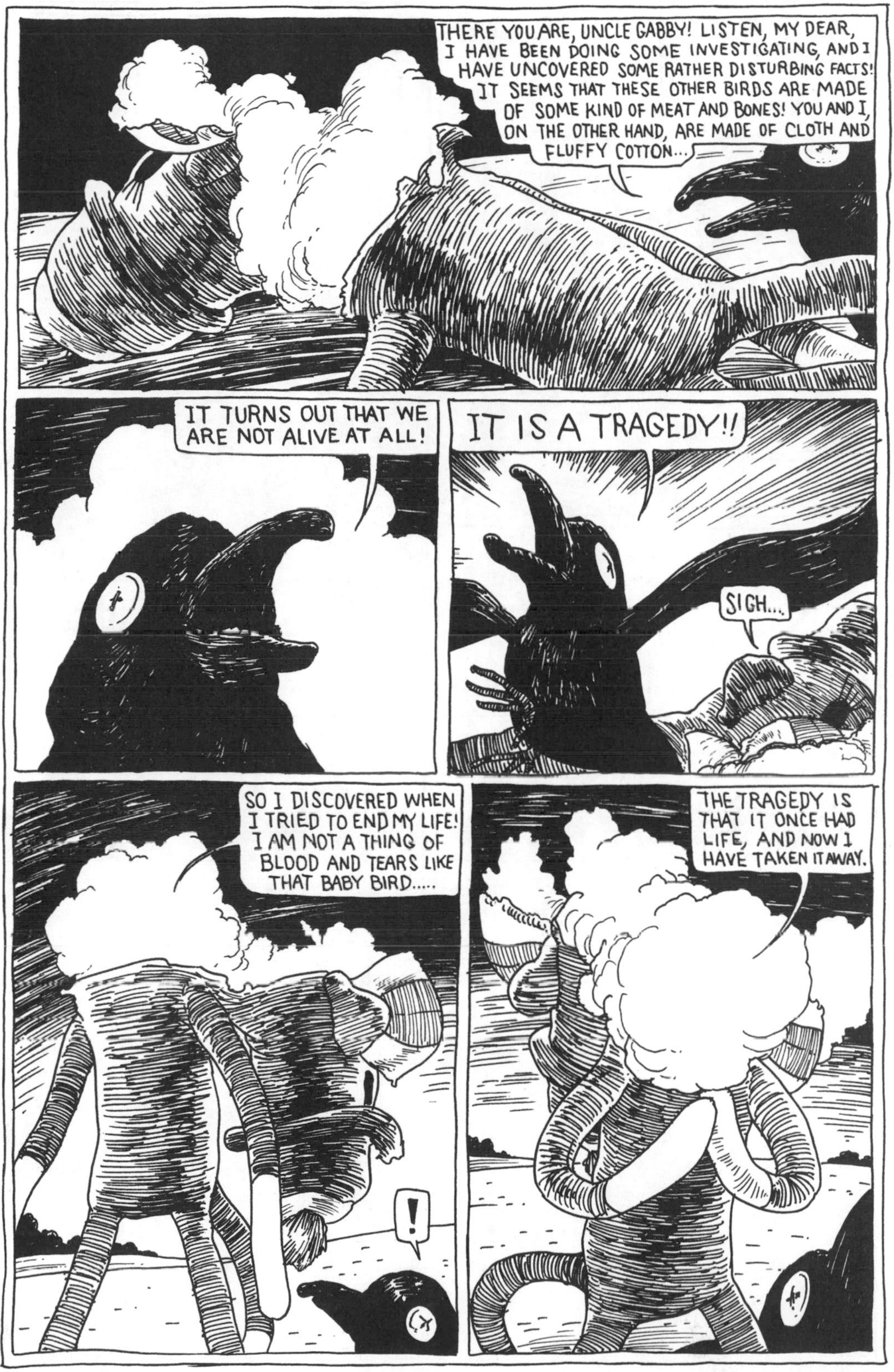
THERE YOU ARE, UNCLE GABBY! LISTEN, MY DEAR, I HAVE BEEN DOING SOME INVESTIGATING, AND I HAVE UNCOVERED SOME RATHER DISTURBING FACTS! IT SEEMS THAT THESE OTHER BIRDS ARE MADE OF SOME KIND OF MEAT AND BONES! YOU AND I, ON THE OTHER HAND, ARE MADE OF CLOTH AND FLUFFY COTTON...
IT TURNS OUT THAT WE ARE NOT ALIVE AT ALL!
IT IS A TRAGEDY!!
SIGH...
SO I DISCOVERED WHEN I TRIED TO END MY LIFE! I AM NOT A THING OF BLOOD AND TEARS LIKE THAT BABY BIRD.....
!
THE TRAGEDY IS THAT IT ONCE HAD LIFE, AND NOW I HAVE TAKEN IT AWAY.

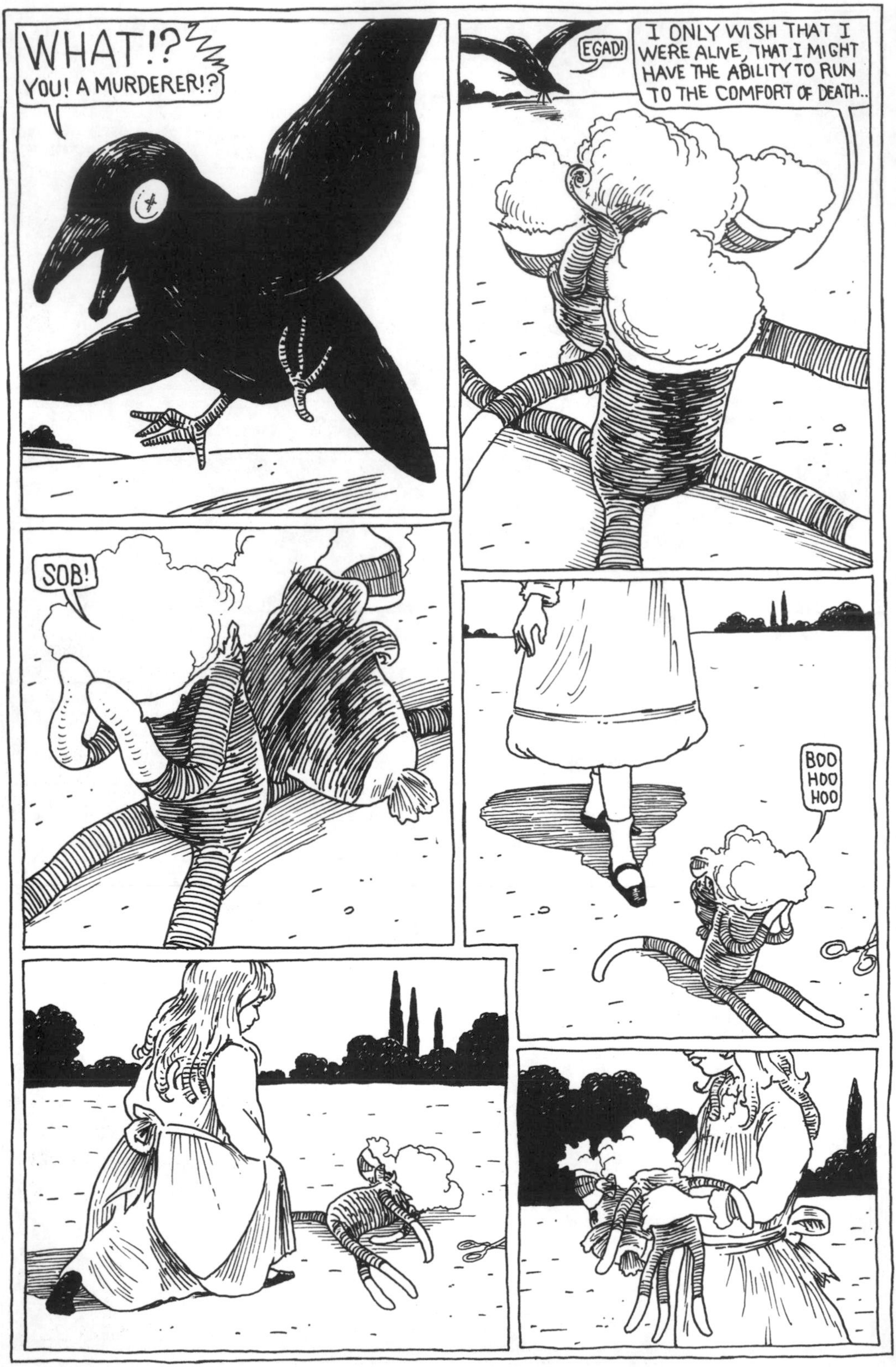
WHAT!?
YOU! A MURDERER!?
EGAD!
I ONLY WISH THAT I WERE ALIVE, THAT I MIGHT HAVE THE ABILITY TO RUN TO THE COMFORT OF DEATH..
SOB!
BOO HOO HOO

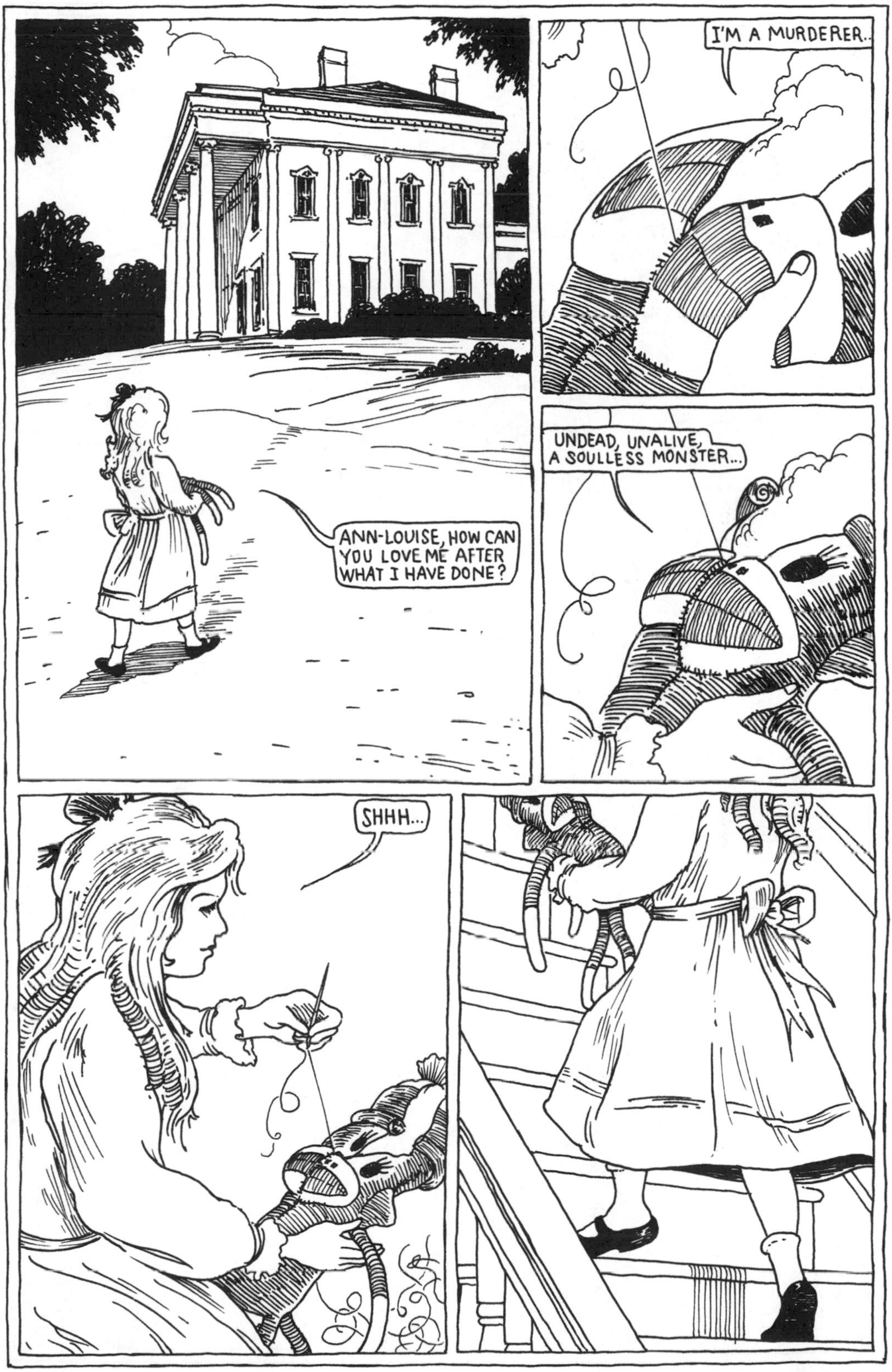
ANN-LOUISE, HOW CAN YOU LOVE ME AFTER WHAT I HAVE DONE?
I'M A MURDERER...
UNDEAD, UNALIVE, A SOULLESS MONSTER...
SHHH...

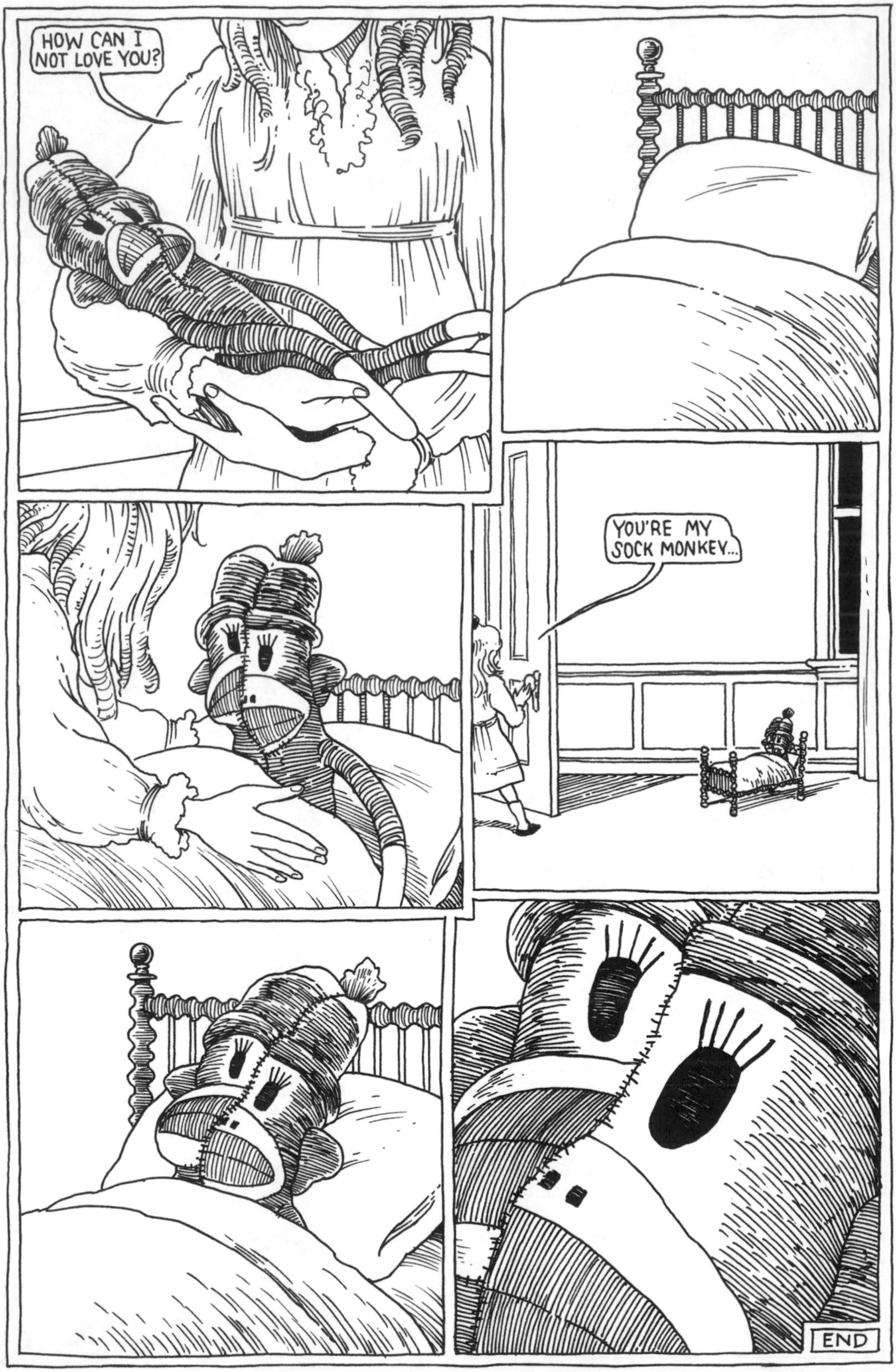
HOW CAN I NOT LOVE YOU?
YOU'RE MY SOCK MONKEY...
END

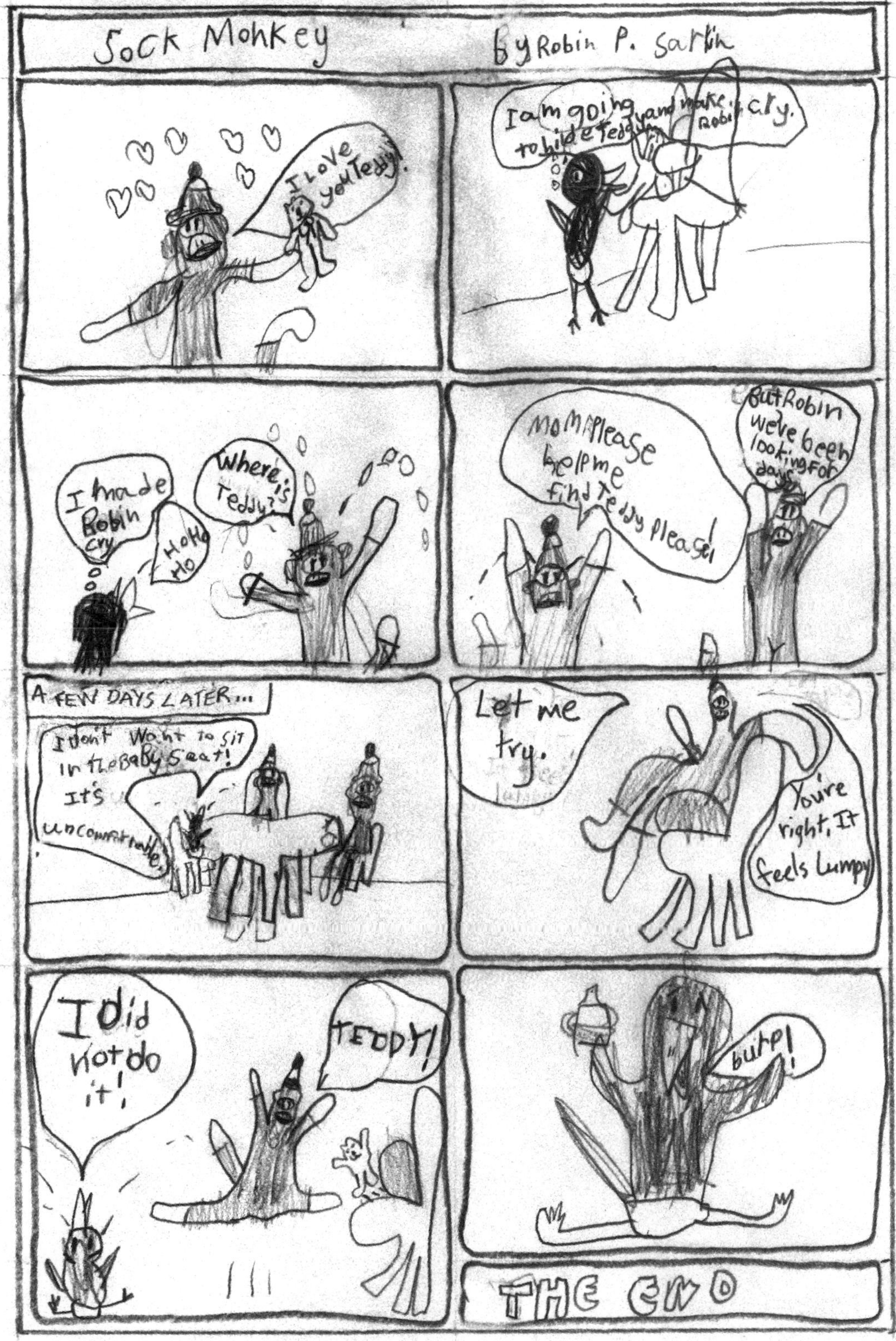
Sock Monkey
by Robin P. Sarkin
I love you Teddy!
I am going to hide Teddy and make Robin cry.
I made Robin cry
Where is Teddy?
HoHo Ho
Mom Please help me find Teddy Please!
But Robin we've been looking for days
A FEW DAYS LATER...
I don't want to sit in the Baby Seat! It's uncomfortable.
Let me try.
You're right, It feels Lumpy
I did not do it!
TEDDY!
burp!
THE END

**RANDY SCUPPER AND Dr. SPANKS**

By TONY MILLIONAIRE

...THE ATTENDANT CIRCUMSTANCES OF PARTURITION...

ETC...

MATERNITY WARD

IT'S THE ANTICIPATION THAT GRATES THE NERVES...

AH! THE PORTAL BECKONS! LIFE AWAITS!

CREAK

GULP! BEING BORN QUICKENS THE HEART!

THROB

WITH MY PRYING PASSION DART I MUST INDUCE THIS UNTAMED HEART TO GRASP THE ART OF LOVE

BITTER APPLE! UGLY FRUIT! SURRENDER SIR! DO NOT EVADE MY KIND PURSUIT!

WHAT THE DEVIL ARE YOU ABOUT, SIR!?

SLAP!

DO YOU PRESUME TO EXPECT ME, RANDALL SCUPPER, ON THE FIRST DAY OF MY HERETOFORE UNLIVED LIFE, TO SUFFER A SLAP!? TO TURN THE OTHER CHEEK? I DEMAND SATISFACTION FOR THE BLOW!!

I HAVE NEVER BEEN MORE DETERMINED TO RECEIVE SATISFACTION IN A REGULAR WAY! I AM A RARE PLUCKED 'UN!!

O WILD AND RAGING SAVAGE LUMP! MY DUTY'S PLAIN! TO PLY MY CUPID'S WEAPONRY AND SOOTHE THE CHOKED AORTAL VEIN!!

SWAT SWAT

GOTCHA

MADAM! YOU ARE THE MOST BEAUTIFUL WOMAN I HAVE EVER SEEN!

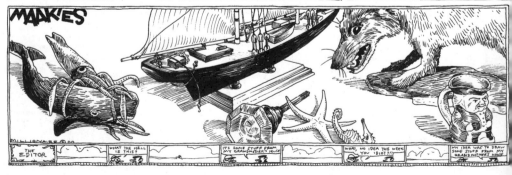

MAAKIES

MILLIONAIRE @ 00

THE EDITOR | WHAT THE HELL IS THIS? | IT'S SOME STUFF FROM MY GRANDMOTHER'S HOUSE | WHAT, NO IDEA THIS WEEK YOU IDIOT?!? | MY IDEA WAS TO DRAW SOME STUFF FROM MY GRANDMOTHER'S HOUSE

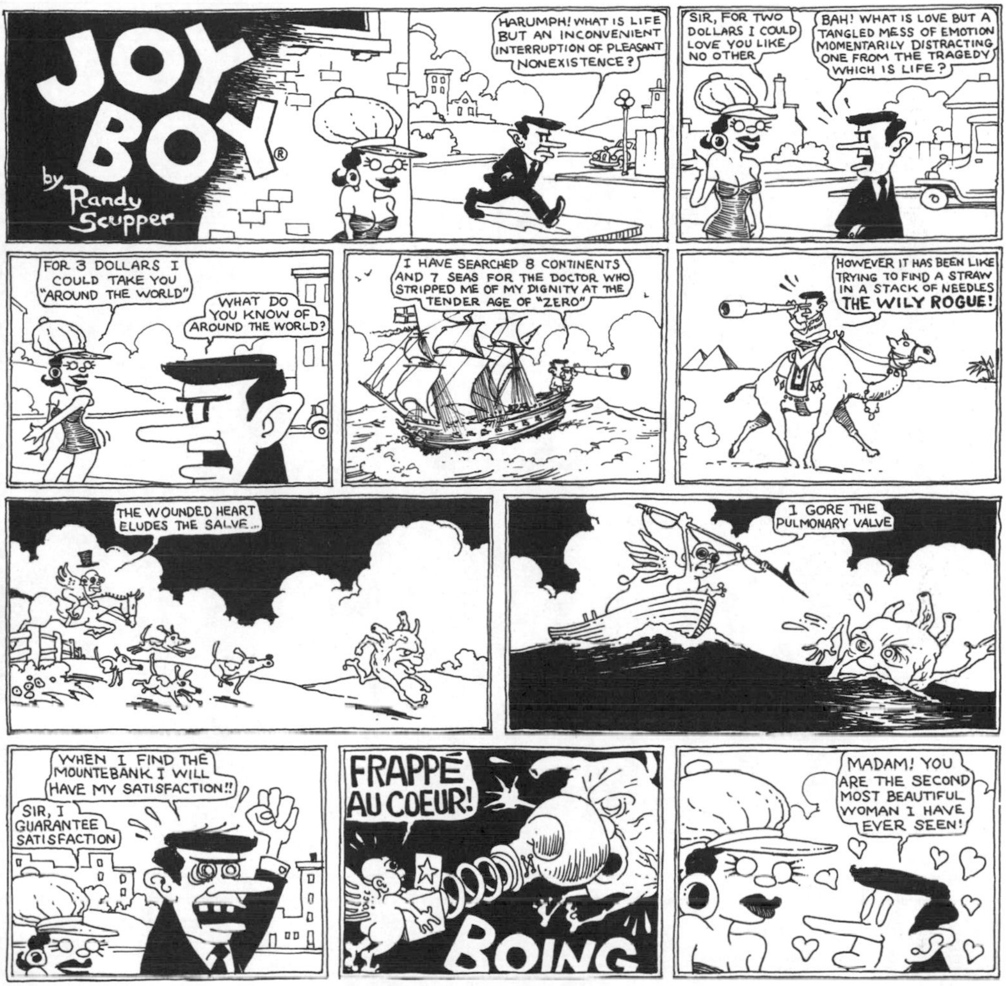
JOY BOY®
by Randy Scupper
HARUMPH! WHAT IS LIFE BUT AN INCONVENIENT INTERRUPTION OF PLEASANT NONEXISTENCE?
SIR, FOR TWO DOLLARS I COULD LOVE YOU LIKE NO OTHER
BAH! WHAT IS LOVE BUT A TANGLED MESS OF EMOTION MOMENTARILY DISTRACTING ONE FROM THE TRAGEDY WHICH IS LIFE?
FOR 3 DOLLARS I COULD TAKE YOU "AROUND THE WORLD"
WHAT DO YOU KNOW OF AROUND THE WORLD?
I HAVE SEARCHED 8 CONTINENTS AND 7 SEAS FOR THE DOCTOR WHO STRIPPED ME OF MY DIGNITY AT THE TENDER AGE OF "ZERO"
HOWEVER IT HAS BEEN LIKE TRYING TO FIND A STRAW IN A STACK OF NEEDLES THE WILY ROGUE!
THE WOUNDED HEART ELUDES THE SALVE...
I GORE THE PULMONARY VALVE
WHEN I FIND THE MOUNTEBANK I WILL HAVE MY SATISFACTION!!
SIR, I GUARANTEE SATISFACTION
FRAPPÉ AU COEUR!
BOING
MADAM! YOU ARE THE SECOND MOST BEAUTIFUL WOMAN I HAVE EVER SEEN!

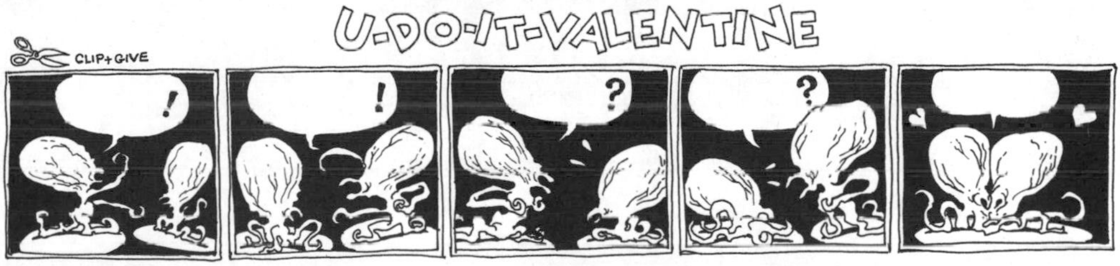
U-DO-IT-VALENTINE
CLIP+GIVE
!
!
?
?

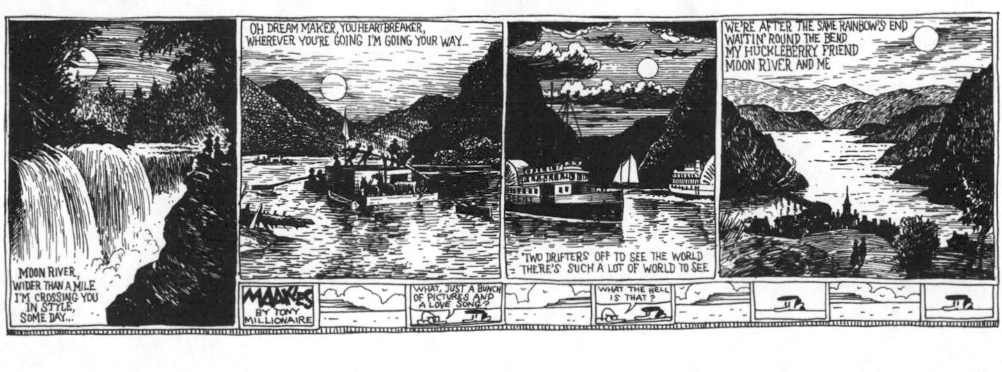
MOON RIVER, WIDER THAN A MILE I'M CROSSING YOU IN STYLE, SOME DAY...
OH DREAM MAKER, YOU HEARTBREAKER, WHEREVER YOU'RE GOING I'M GOING YOUR WAY...
TWO DRIFTERS OFF TO SEE THE WORLD THERE'S SUCH A LOT OF WORLD TO SEE
WE'RE AFTER THE SAME RAINBOW'S END WAITIN' ROUND THE BEND MY HUCKLEBERRY FRIEND MOON RIVER AND ME
MAAKIES BY TONY MILLIONAIRE
WHAT, JUST A BUNCH OF PICTURES AND A LOVE SONG?
WHAT THE HELL IS THAT?

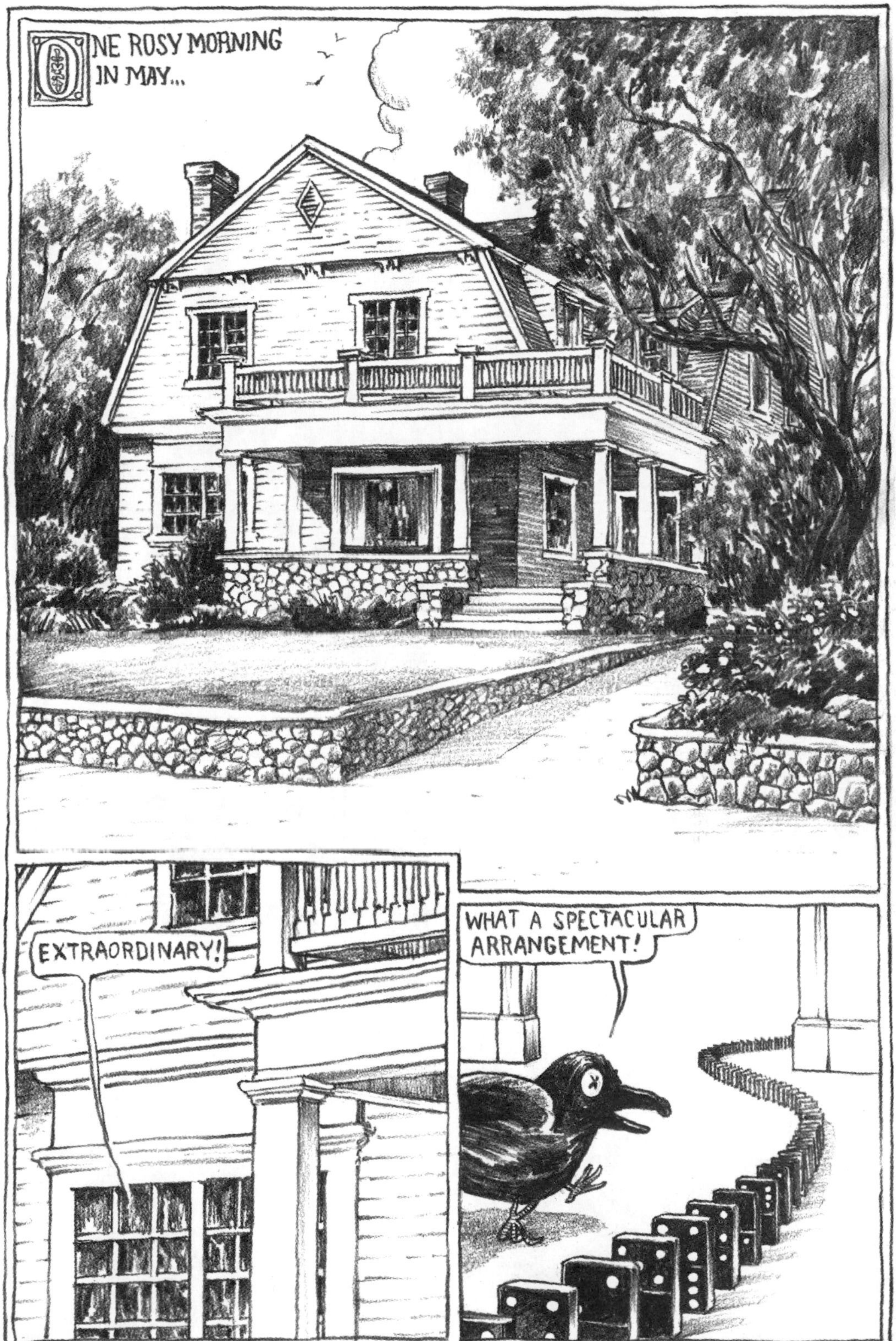
ONE ROSY MORNING IN MAY...
EXTRAORDINARY!
WHAT A SPECTACULAR ARRANGEMENT!

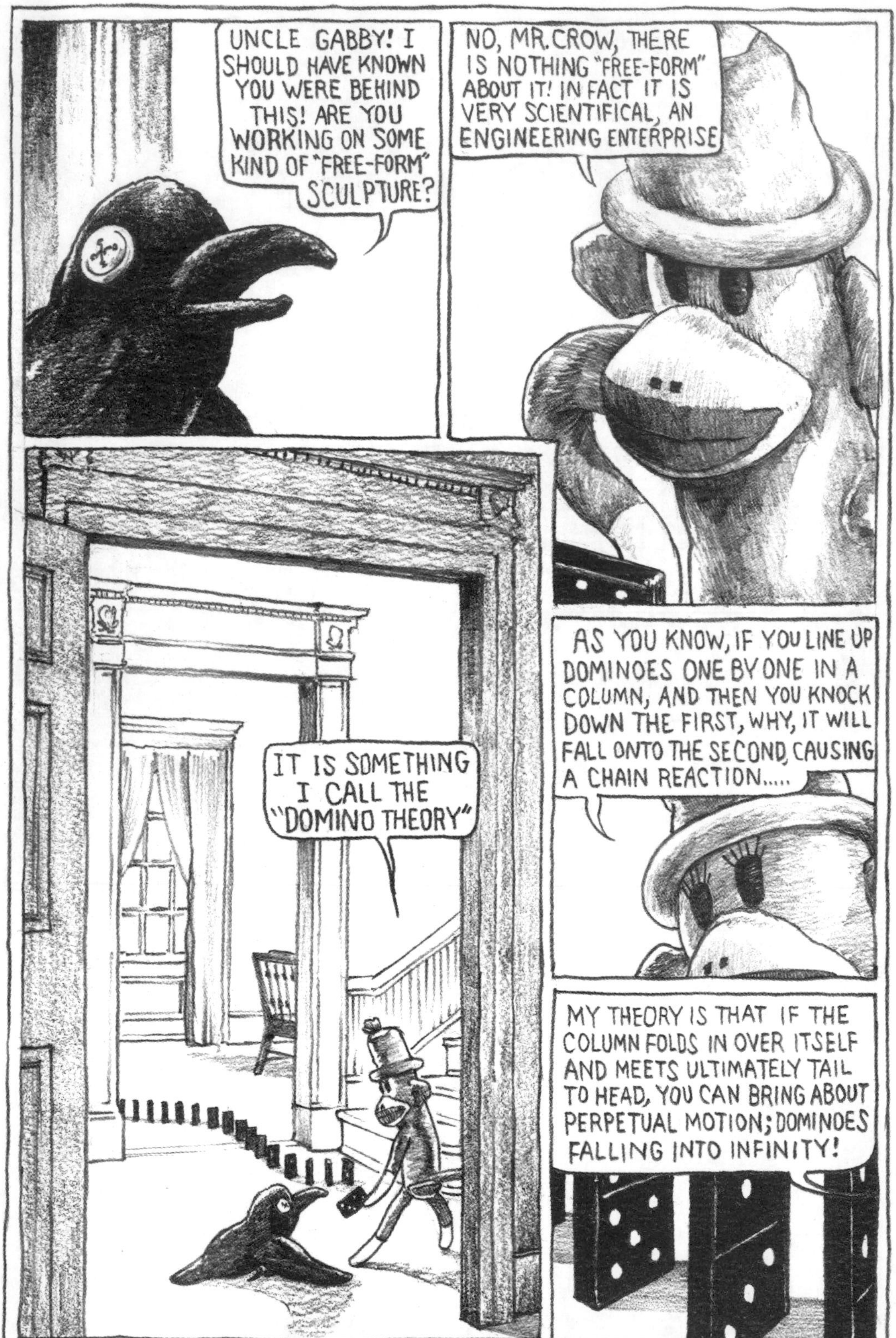
UNCLE GABBY! I SHOULD HAVE KNOWN YOU WERE BEHIND THIS! ARE YOU WORKING ON SOME KIND OF "FREE-FORM" SCULPTURE?
NO, MR. CROW, THERE IS NOTHING "FREE-FORM" ABOUT IT! IN FACT IT IS VERY SCIENTIFICAL, AN ENGINEERING ENTERPRISE
IT IS SOMETHING I CALL THE "DOMINO THEORY"
AS YOU KNOW, IF YOU LINE UP DOMINOES ONE BY ONE IN A COLUMN, AND THEN YOU KNOCK DOWN THE FIRST, WHY, IT WILL FALL ONTO THE SECOND, CAUSING A CHAIN REACTION.....
MY THEORY IS THAT IF THE COLUMN FOLDS IN OVER ITSELF AND MEETS ULTIMATELY TAIL TO HEAD, YOU CAN BRING ABOUT PERPETUAL MOTION; DOMINOES FALLING INTO INFINITY!

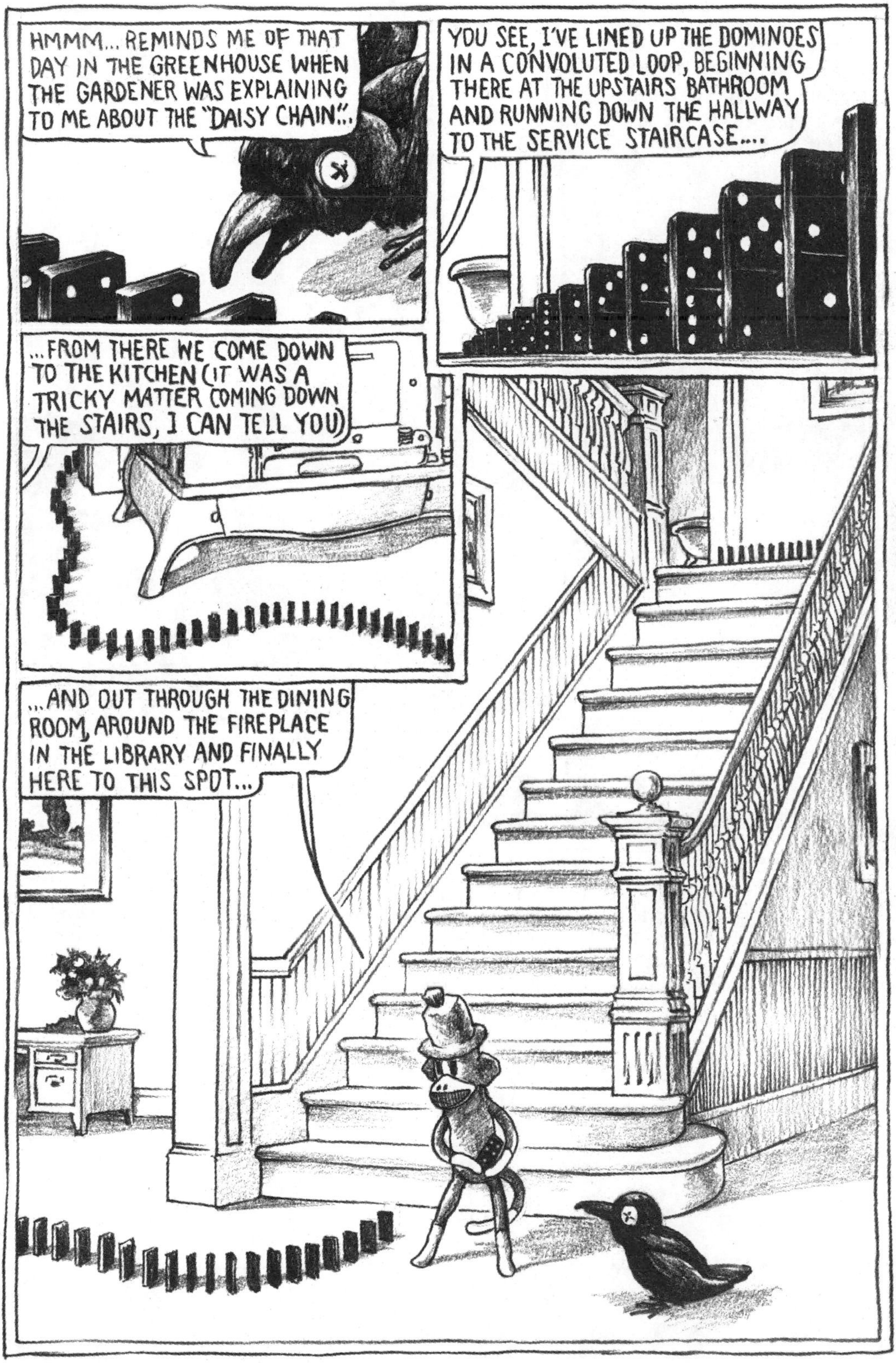
HMMM... REMINDS ME OF THAT DAY IN THE GREENHOUSE WHEN THE GARDENER WAS EXPLAINING TO ME ABOUT THE "DAISY CHAIN"...
YOU SEE, I'VE LINED UP THE DOMINOES IN A CONVOLUTED LOOP, BEGINNING THERE AT THE UPSTAIRS BATHROOM AND RUNNING DOWN THE HALLWAY TO THE SERVICE STAIRCASE....
...FROM THERE WE COME DOWN TO THE KITCHEN (IT WAS A TRICKY MATTER COMING DOWN THE STAIRS, I CAN TELL YOU)
...AND OUT THROUGH THE DINING ROOM, AROUND THE FIREPLACE IN THE LIBRARY AND FINALLY HERE TO THIS SPOT...

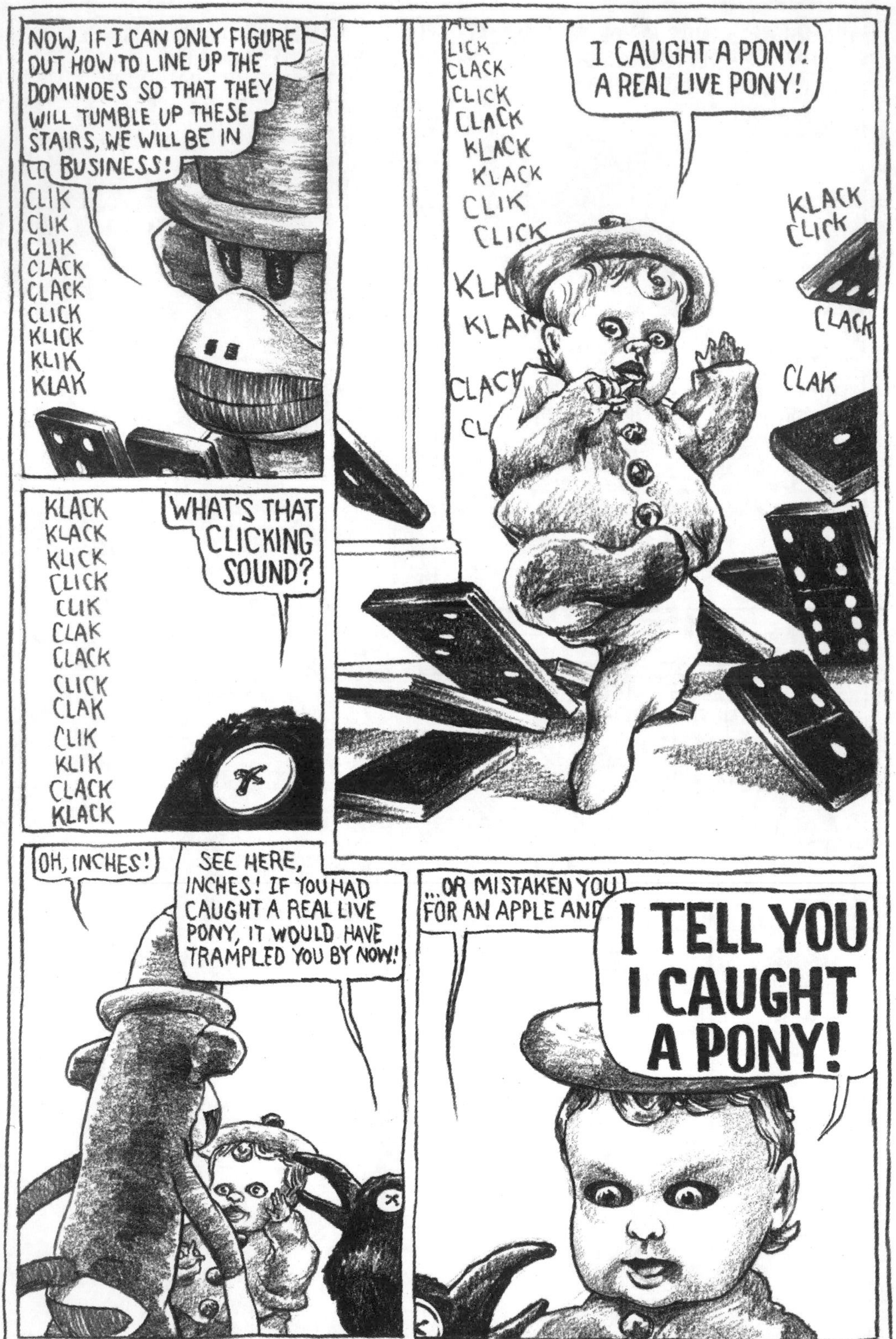
NOW, IF I CAN ONLY FIGURE OUT HOW TO LINE UP THE DOMINOES SO THAT THEY WILL TUMBLE UP THESE STAIRS, WE WILL BE IN BUSINESS!
CLIK
CLIK
CLIK
CLACK
CLACK
CLICK
KLICK
KLIK
KLAK
KLACK
KLACK
KLICK
CLICK
CLIK
CLAK
CLACK
CLICK
CLAK
CLIK
KLIK
CLACK
KLACK
WHAT'S THAT CLICKING SOUND?
LICK
CLACK
CLICK
CLACK
KLACK
KLACK
CLIK
CLICK
I CAUGHT A PONY! A REAL LIVE PONY!
KLACK
CLICK
CLACK
CLAK
KLAK
CLACK
OH, INCHES!
SEE HERE, INCHES! IF YOU HAD CAUGHT A REAL LIVE PONY, IT WOULD HAVE TRAMPLED YOU BY NOW!
...OR MISTAKEN YOU FOR AN APPLE AND
I TELL YOU I CAUGHT A PONY!

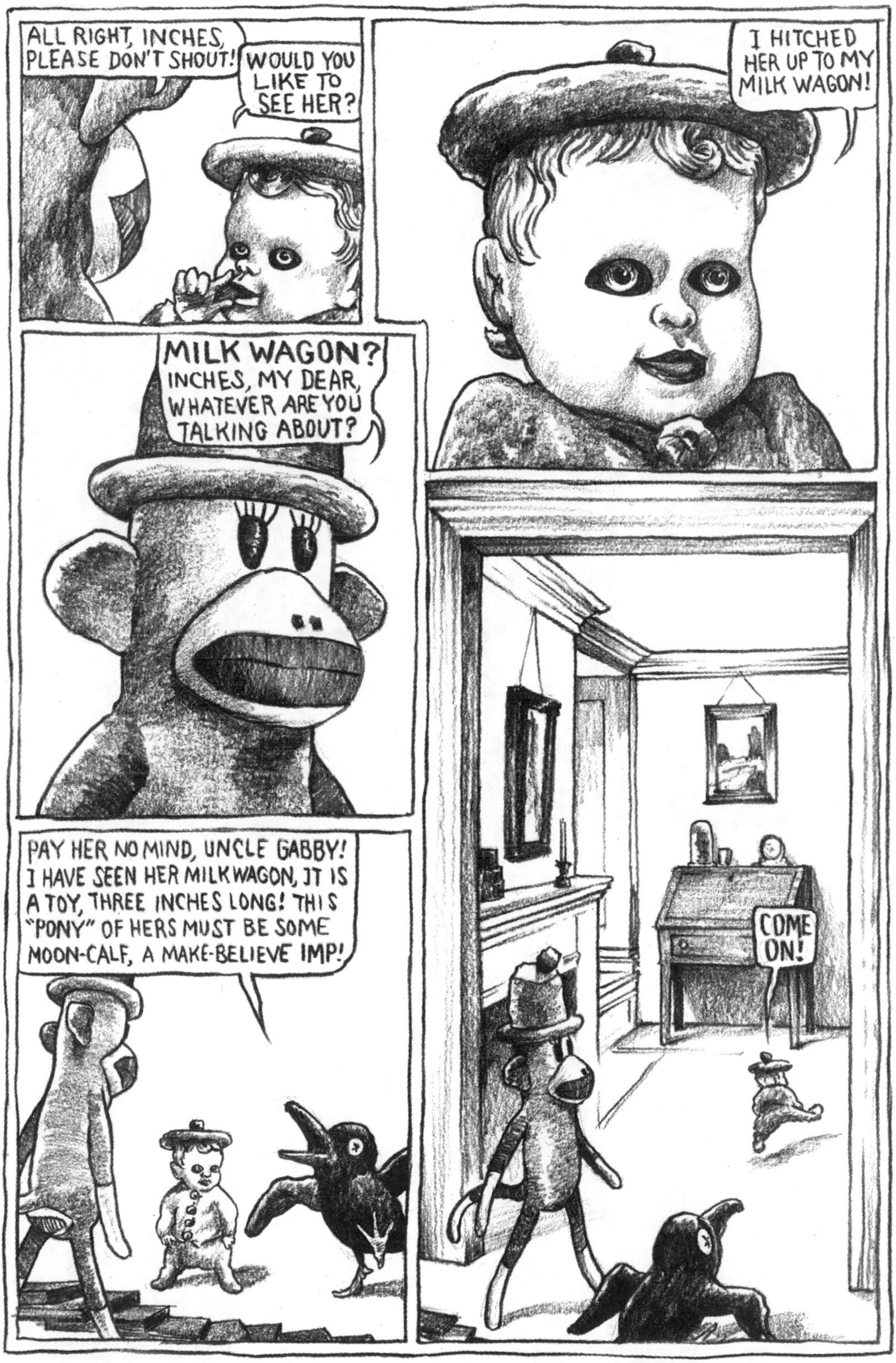
ALL RIGHT, INCHES, PLEASE DON'T SHOUT!
WOULD YOU LIKE TO SEE HER?
I HITCHED HER UP TO MY MILK WAGON!
MILK WAGON? INCHES, MY DEAR, WHATEVER ARE YOU TALKING ABOUT?
PAY HER NO MIND, UNCLE GABBY! I HAVE SEEN HER MILKWAGON, IT IS A TOY, THREE INCHES LONG! THIS "PONY" OF HERS MUST BE SOME MOON-CALF, A MAKE-BELIEVE IMP!
COME ON!

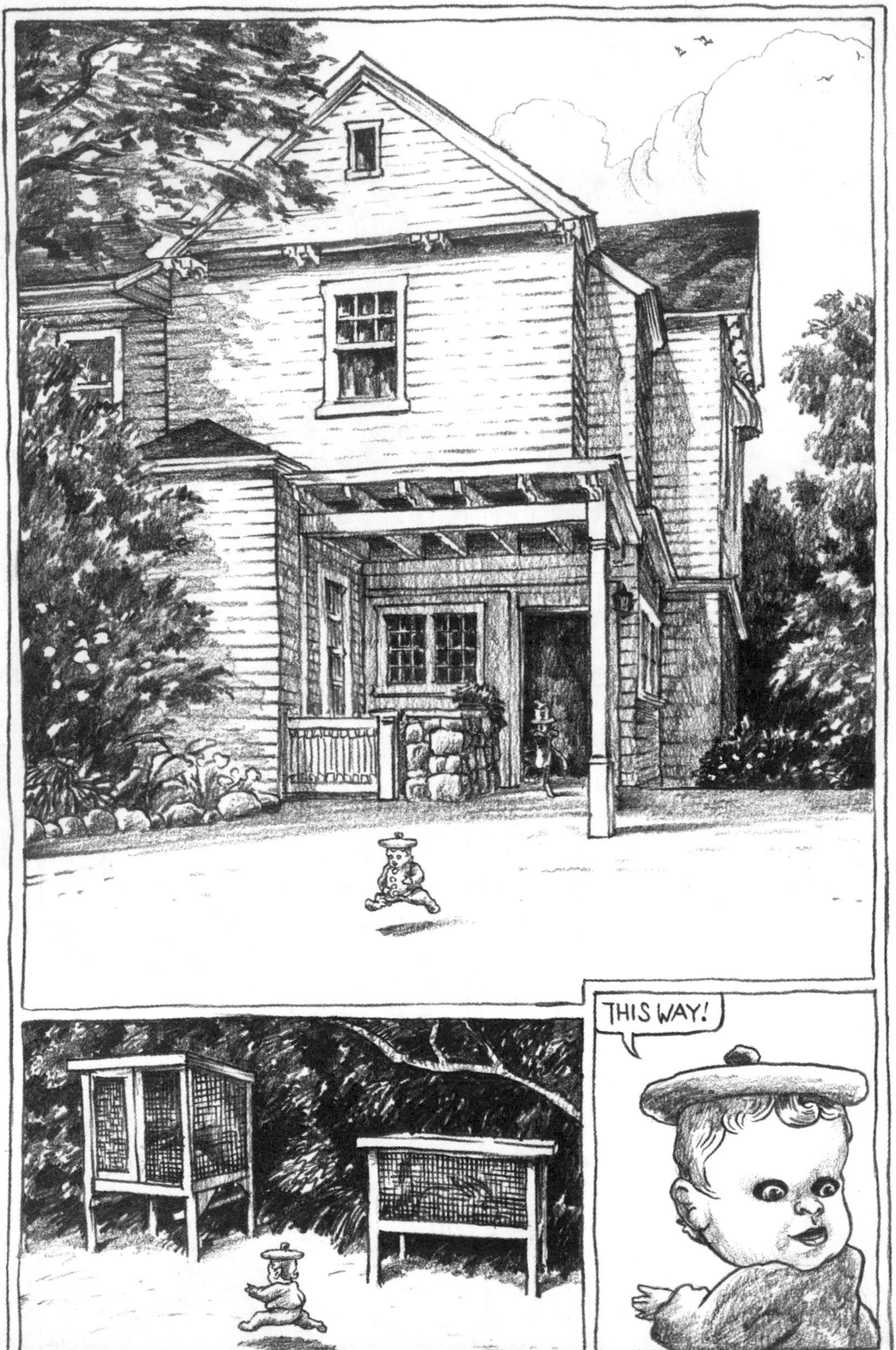
THIS WAY!

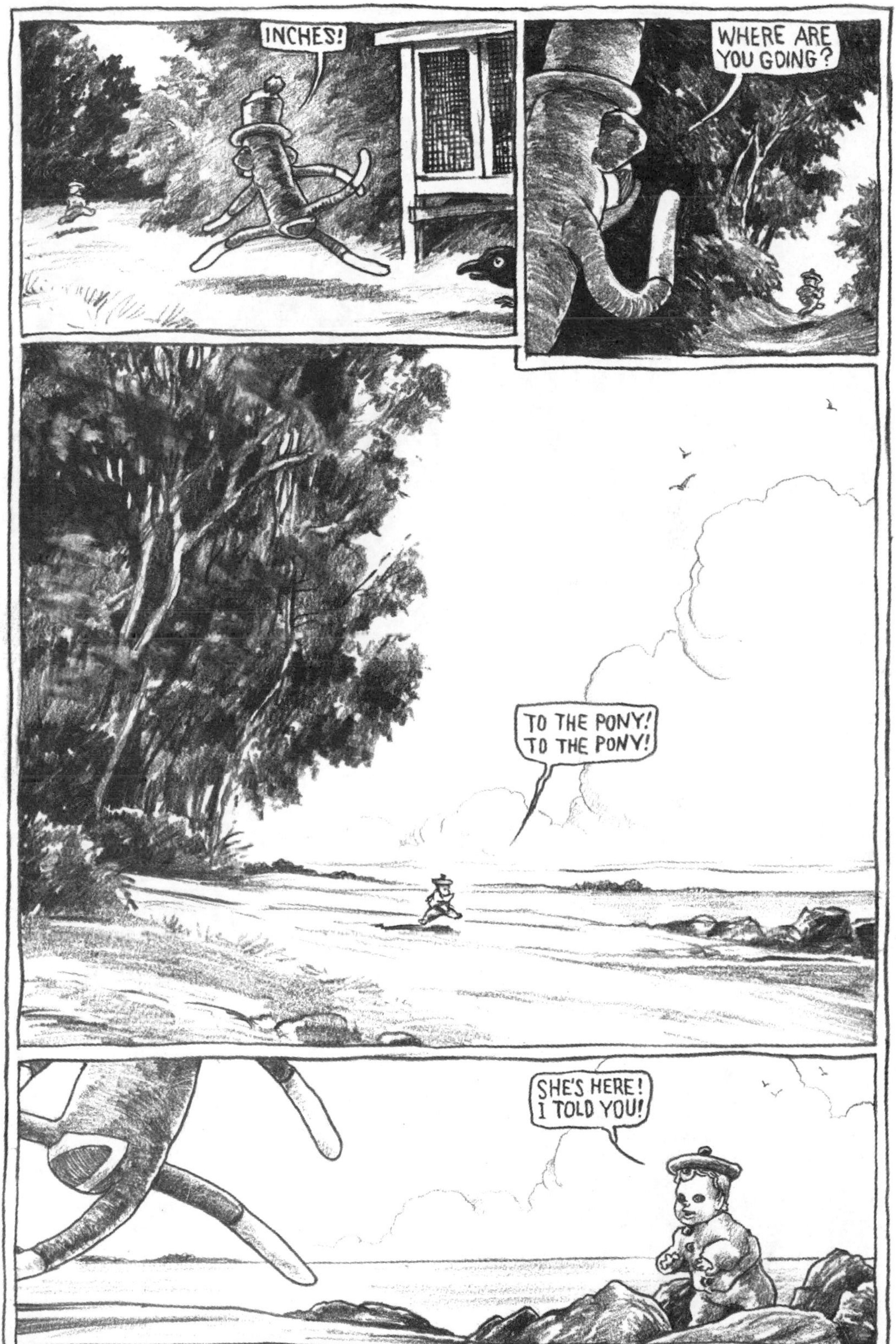
INCHES!
WHERE ARE YOU GOING?
TO THE PONY! TO THE PONY!
SHE'S HERE! I TOLD YOU!

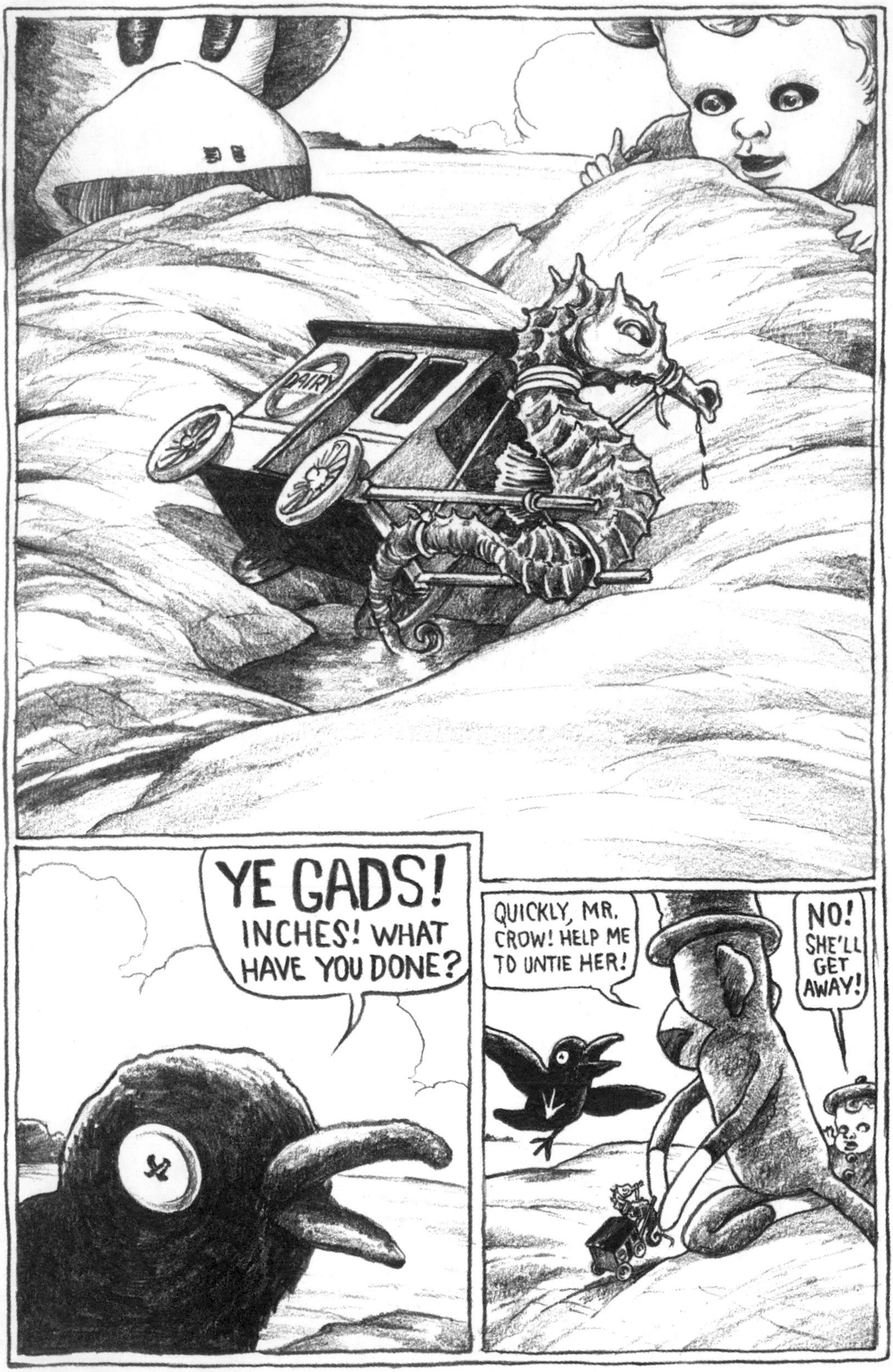
DAIRY
YE GADS! INCHES! WHAT HAVE YOU DONE?
QUICKLY, MR. CROW! HELP ME TO UNTIE HER!
NO! SHE'LL GET AWAY!

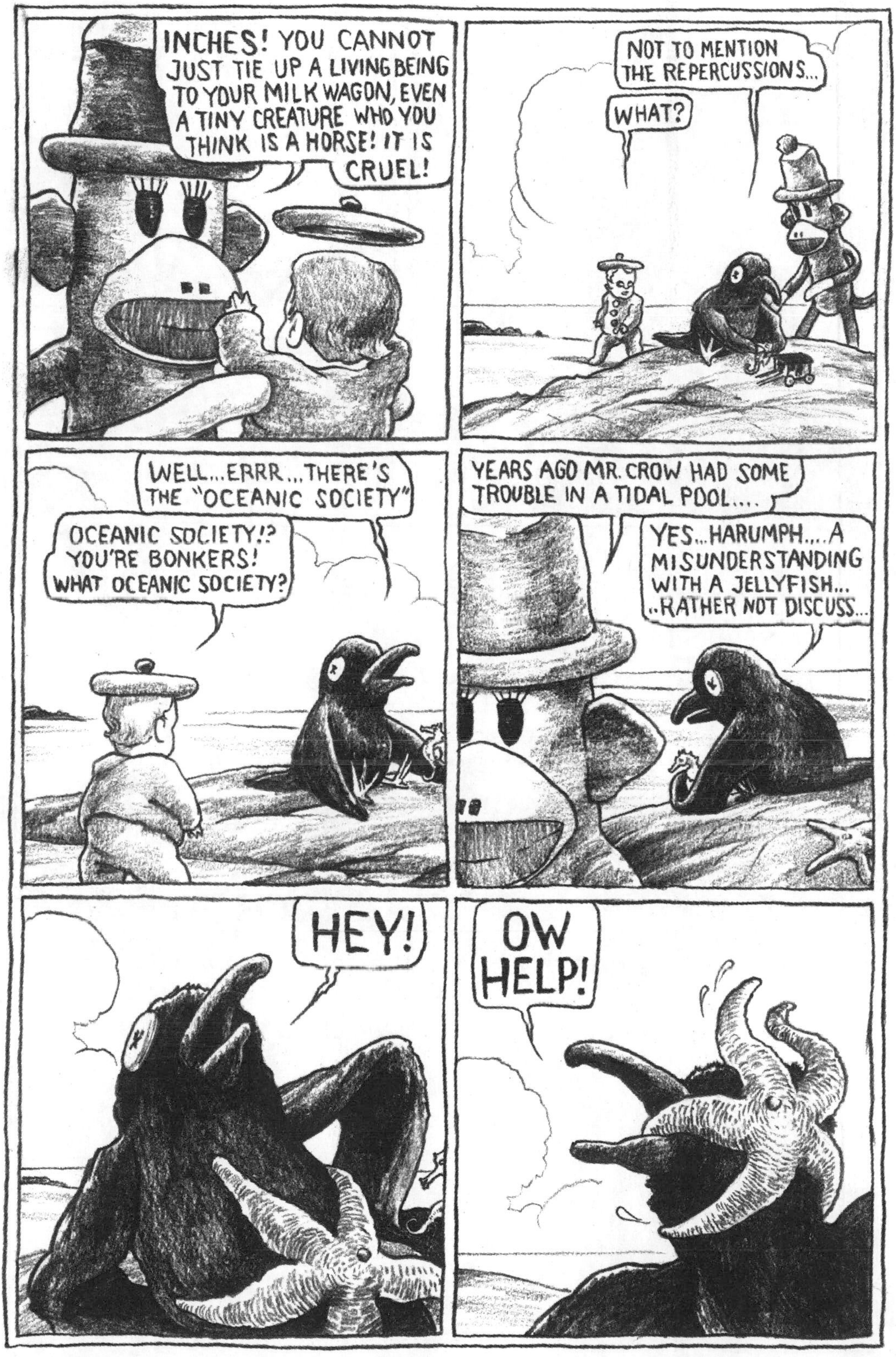
INCHES! YOU CANNOT JUST TIE UP A LIVING BEING TO YOUR MILK WAGON, EVEN A TINY CREATURE WHO YOU THINK IS A HORSE! IT IS CRUEL!
NOT TO MENTION THE REPERCUSSIONS...
WHAT?
WELL...ERRR..., THERE'S THE "OCEANIC SOCIETY"
OCEANIC SOCIETY!? YOU'RE BONKERS! WHAT OCEANIC SOCIETY?
YEARS AGO MR. CROW HAD SOME TROUBLE IN A TIDAL POOL....
YES...HARUMPH.....A MISUNDERSTANDING WITH A JELLYFISH... ..RATHER NOT DISCUSS...
HEY!
OW HELP!

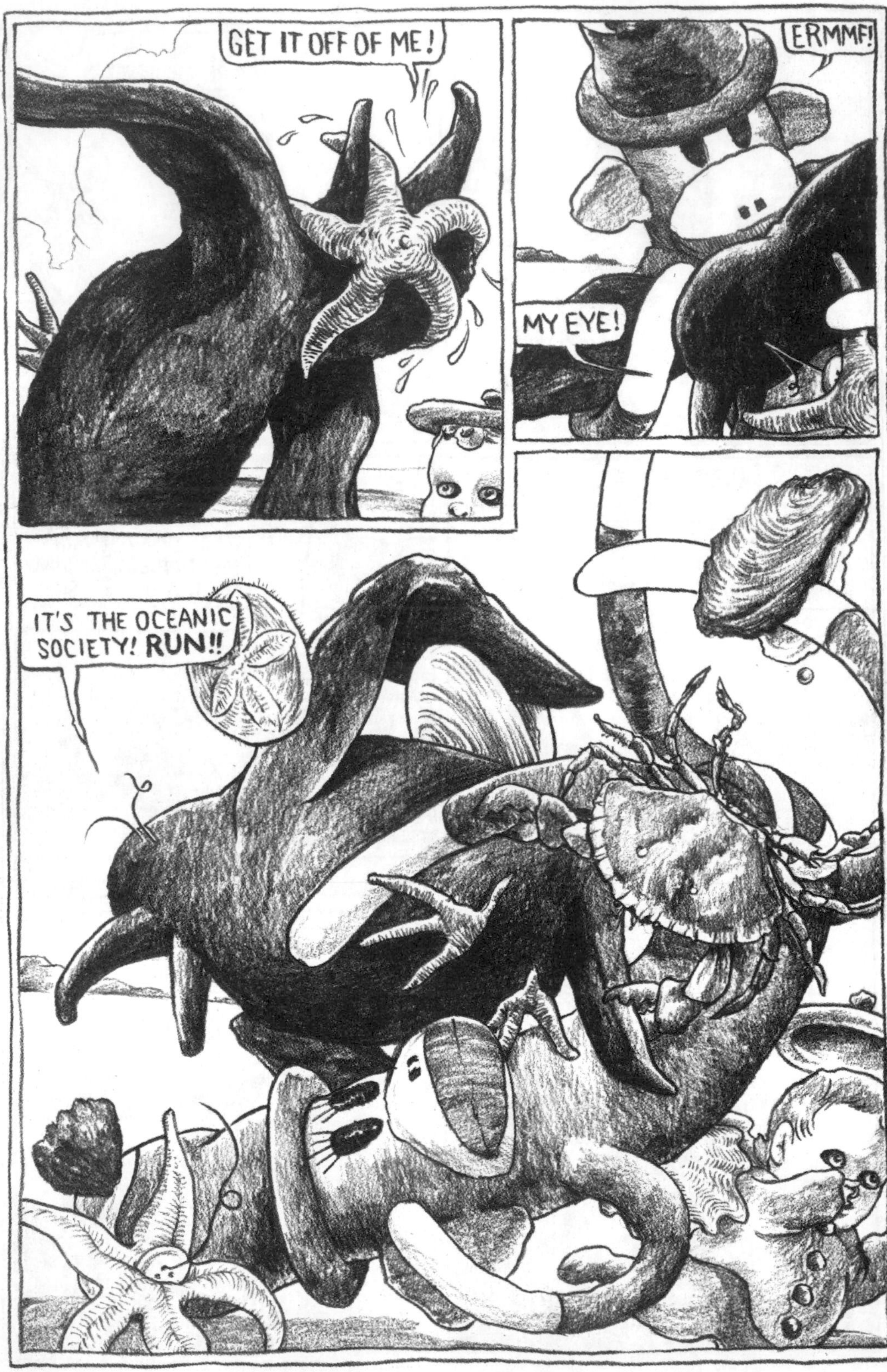
GET IT OFF OF ME!
ERMMF!
MY EYE!
IT'S THE OCEANIC SOCIETY! **RUN!!**

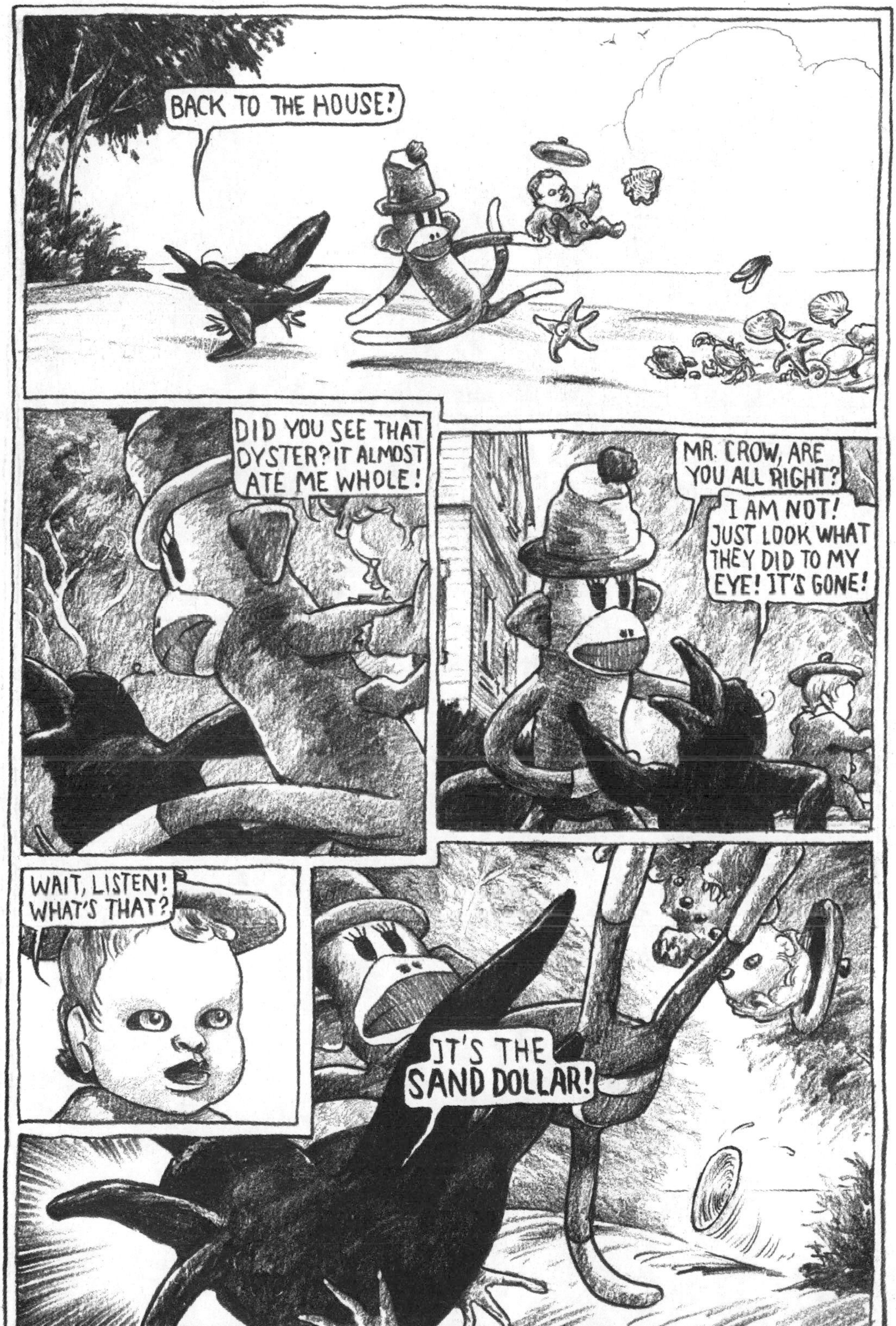
BACK TO THE HOUSE!
DID YOU SEE THAT OYSTER? IT ALMOST ATE ME WHOLE!
MR. CROW, ARE YOU ALL RIGHT?
I AM NOT! JUST LOOK WHAT THEY DID TO MY EYE! IT'S GONE!
WAIT, LISTEN! WHAT'S THAT?
IT'S THE SAND DOLLAR!

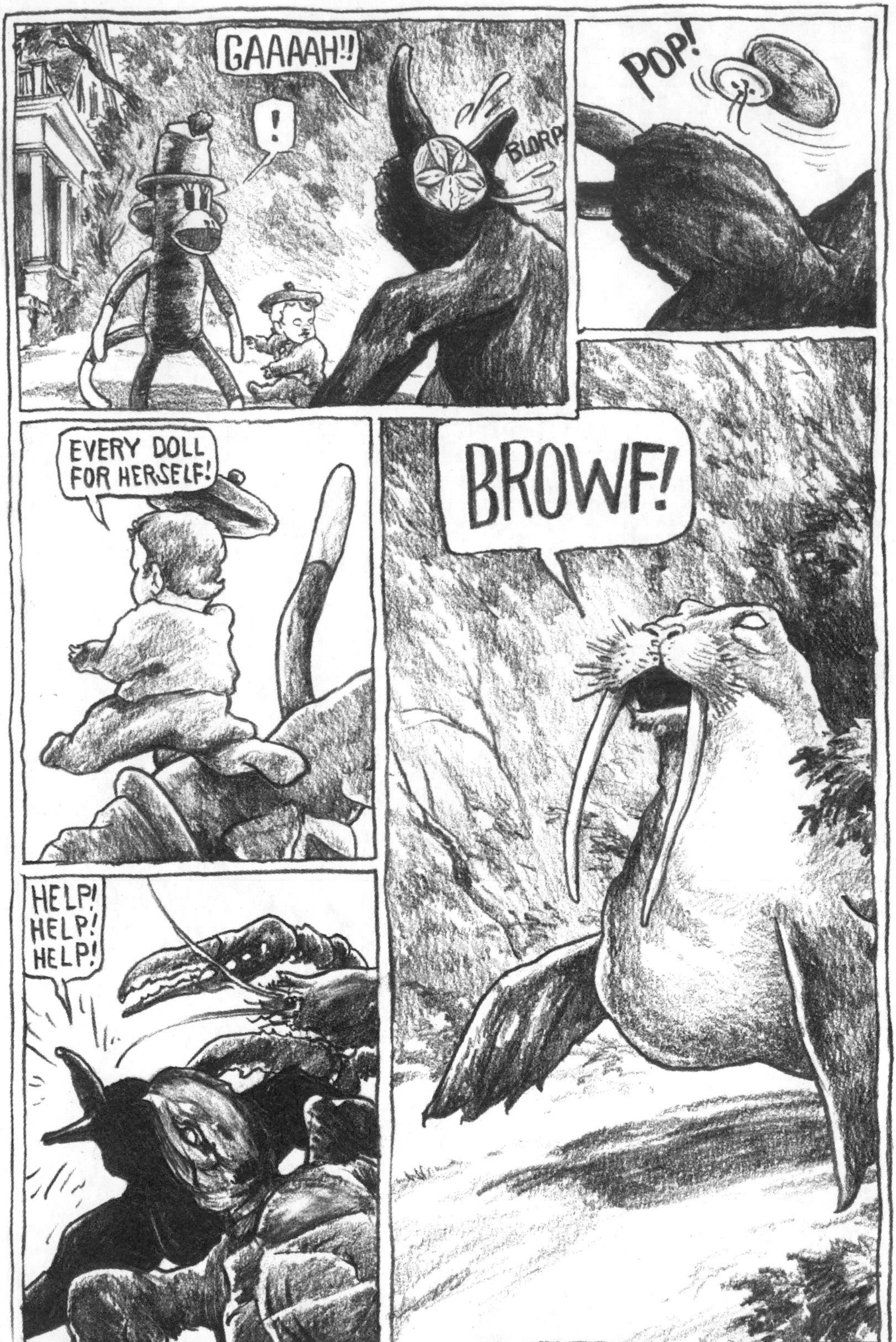
GAAAAH!!
!
BLORP!
POP!
EVERY DOLL FOR HERSELF!
HELP! HELP! HELP!
BROWF!

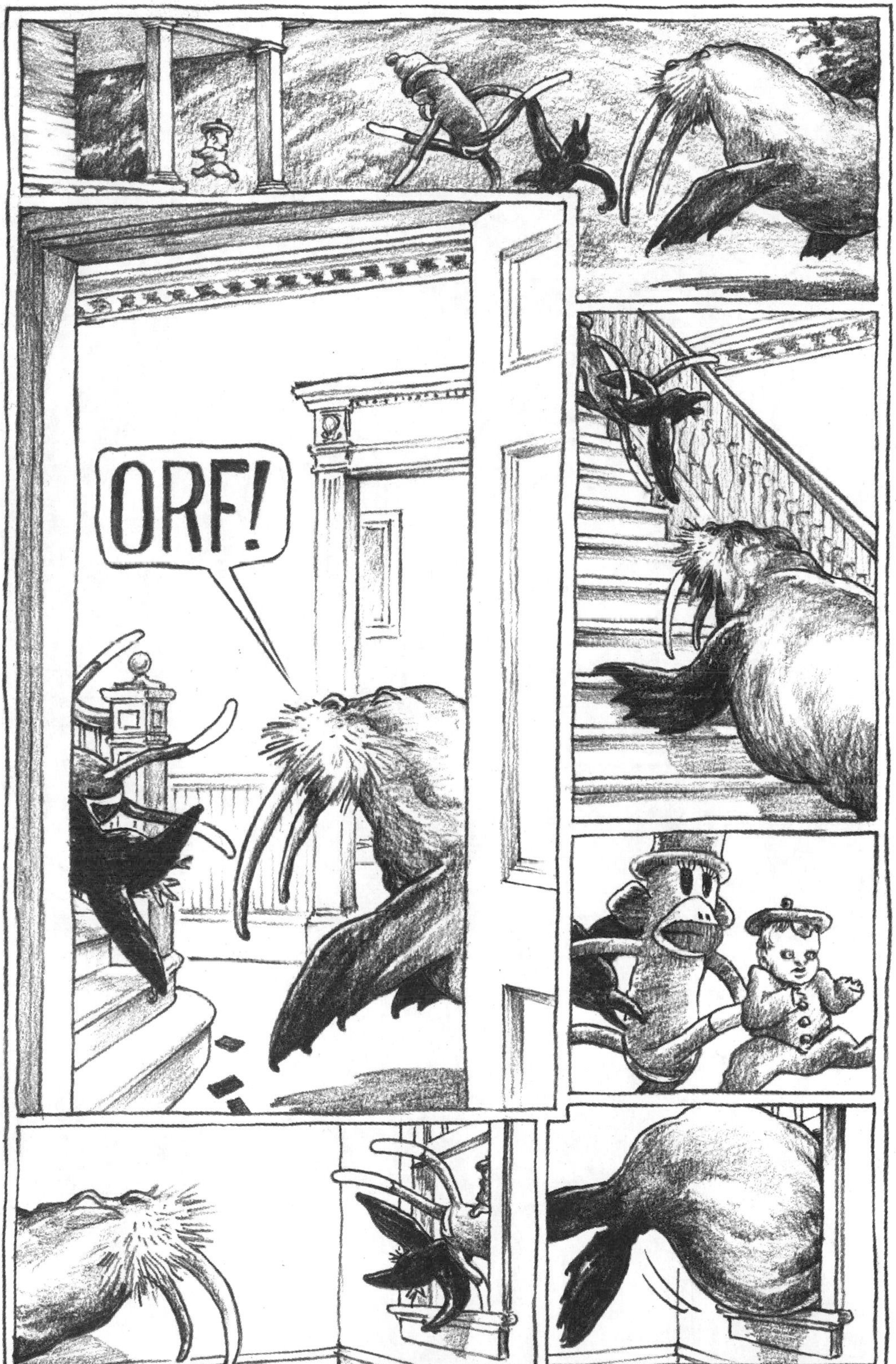
ORF!

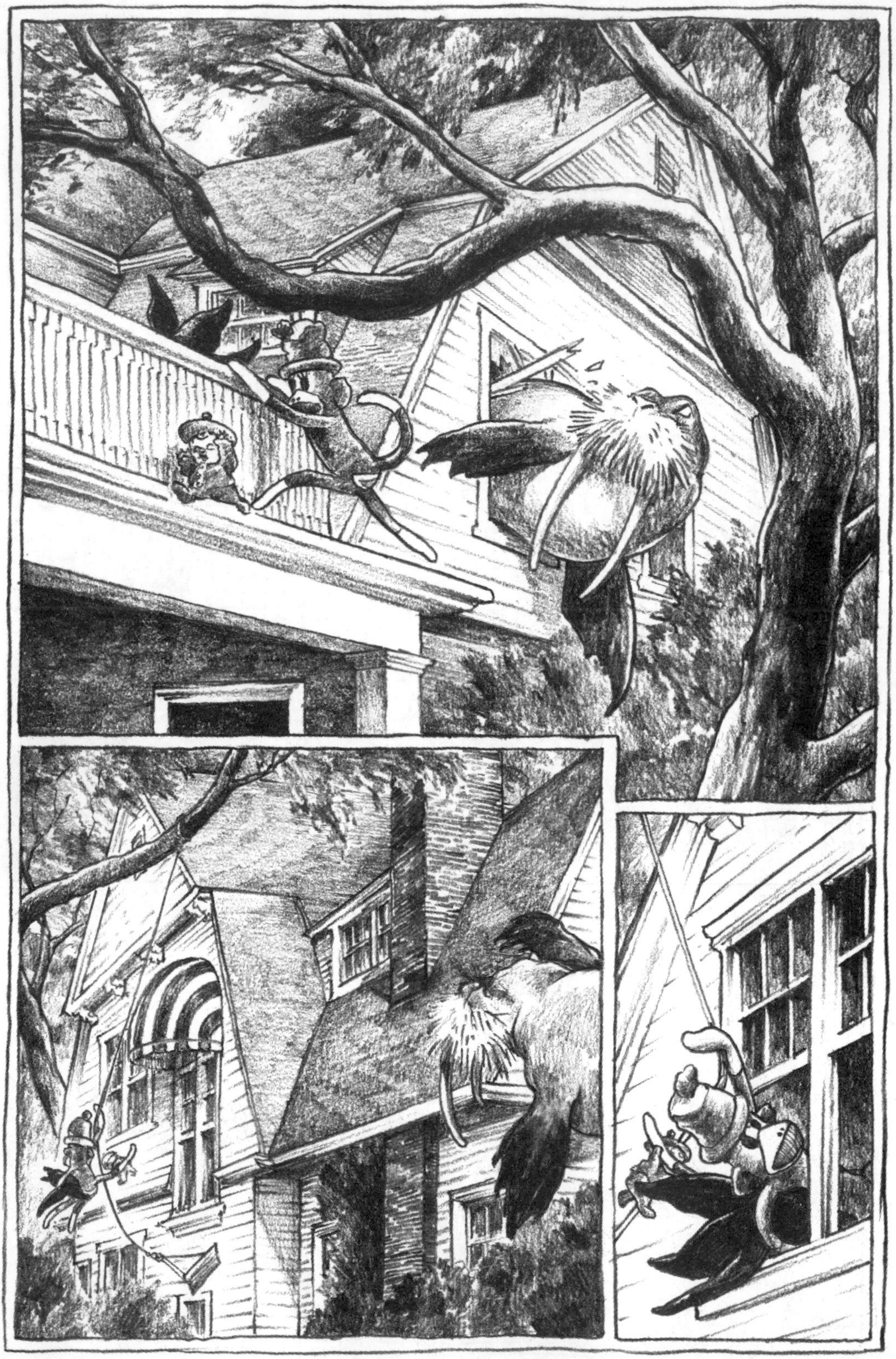

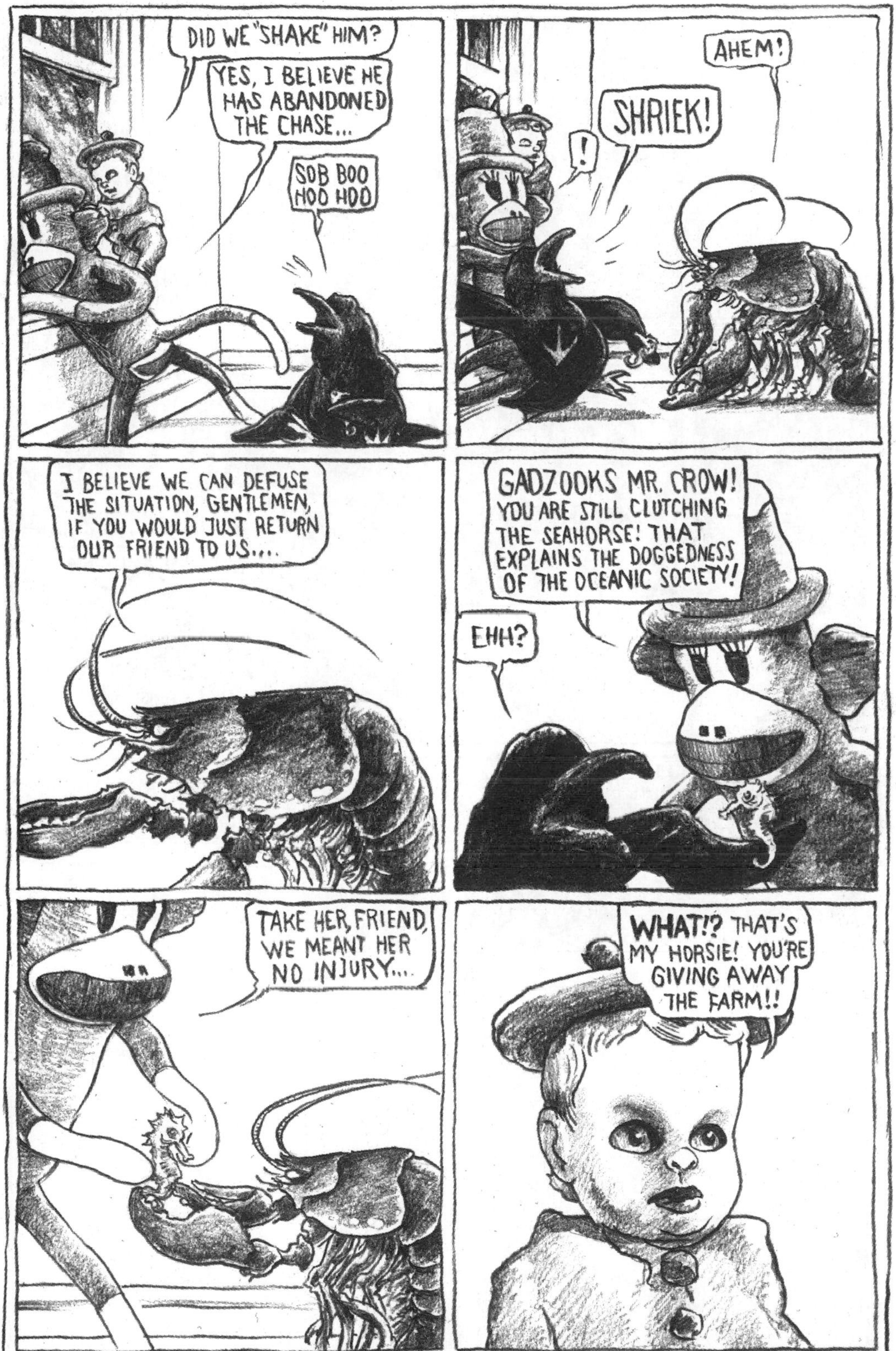
DID WE "SHAKE" HIM?
YES, I BELIEVE HE HAS ABANDONED THE CHASE...
SOB BOO HOO HOO
AHEM!
SHRIEK!
!
I BELIEVE WE CAN DEFUSE THE SITUATION, GENTLEMEN, IF YOU WOULD JUST RETURN OUR FRIEND TO US....
GADZOOKS MR. CROW! YOU ARE STILL CLUTCHING THE SEAHORSE! THAT EXPLAINS THE DOGGEDNESS OF THE OCEANIC SOCIETY!
EHH?
TAKE HER, FRIEND, WE MEANT HER NO INJURY...
WHAT!? THAT'S MY HORSIE! YOU'RE GIVING AWAY THE FARM!!

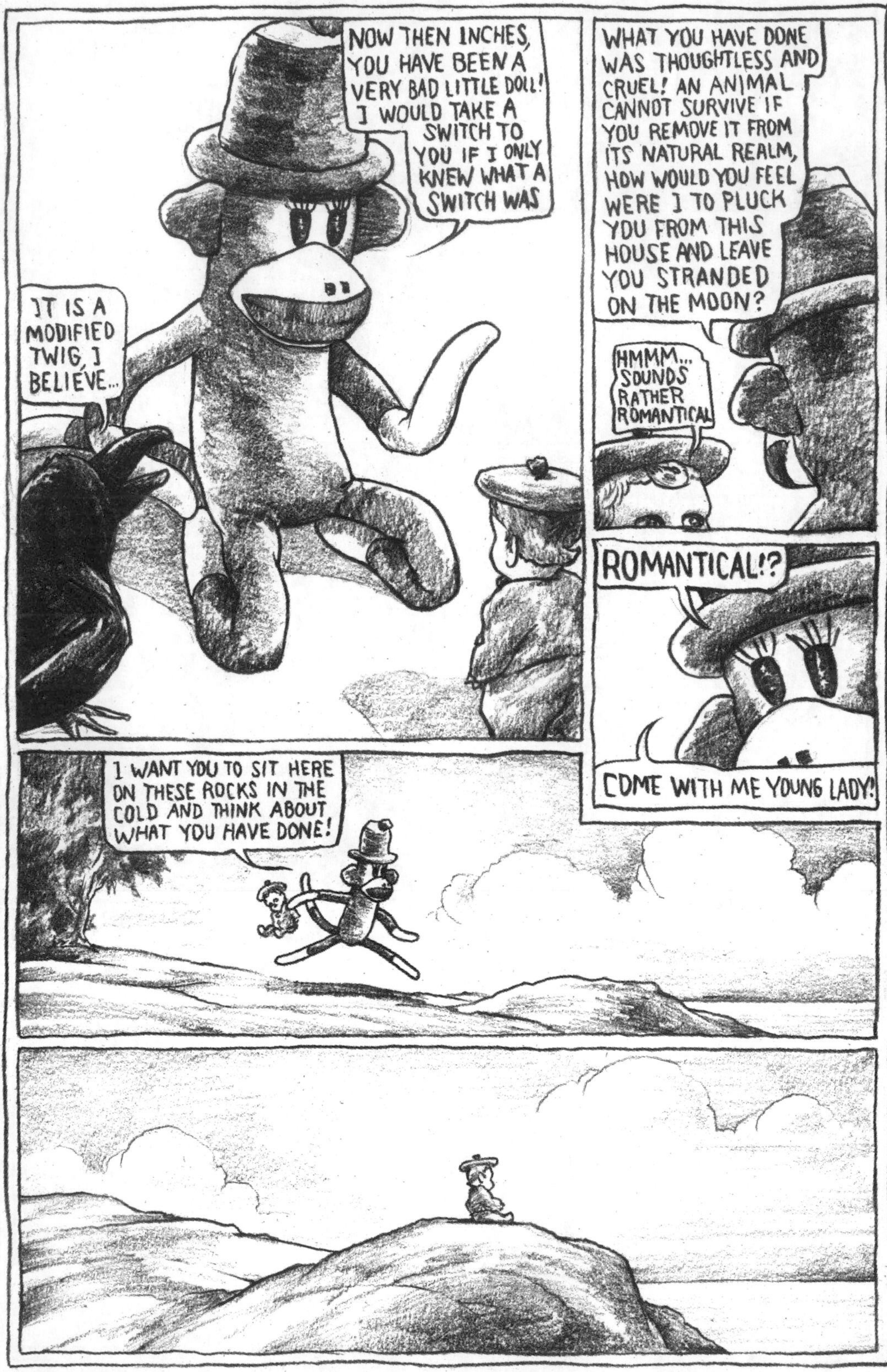
NOW THEN INCHES, YOU HAVE BEEN A VERY BAD LITTLE DOLL! I WOULD TAKE A SWITCH TO YOU IF I ONLY KNEW WHAT A SWITCH WAS
IT IS A MODIFIED TWIG, I BELIEVE...
WHAT YOU HAVE DONE WAS THOUGHTLESS AND CRUEL! AN ANIMAL CANNOT SURVIVE IF YOU REMOVE IT FROM ITS NATURAL REALM, HOW WOULD YOU FEEL WERE I TO PLUCK YOU FROM THIS HOUSE AND LEAVE YOU STRANDED ON THE MOON?
HMMM... SOUNDS RATHER ROMANTICAL
ROMANTICAL!?
COME WITH ME YOUNG LADY!
I WANT YOU TO SIT HERE ON THESE ROCKS IN THE COLD AND THINK ABOUT WHAT YOU HAVE DONE!

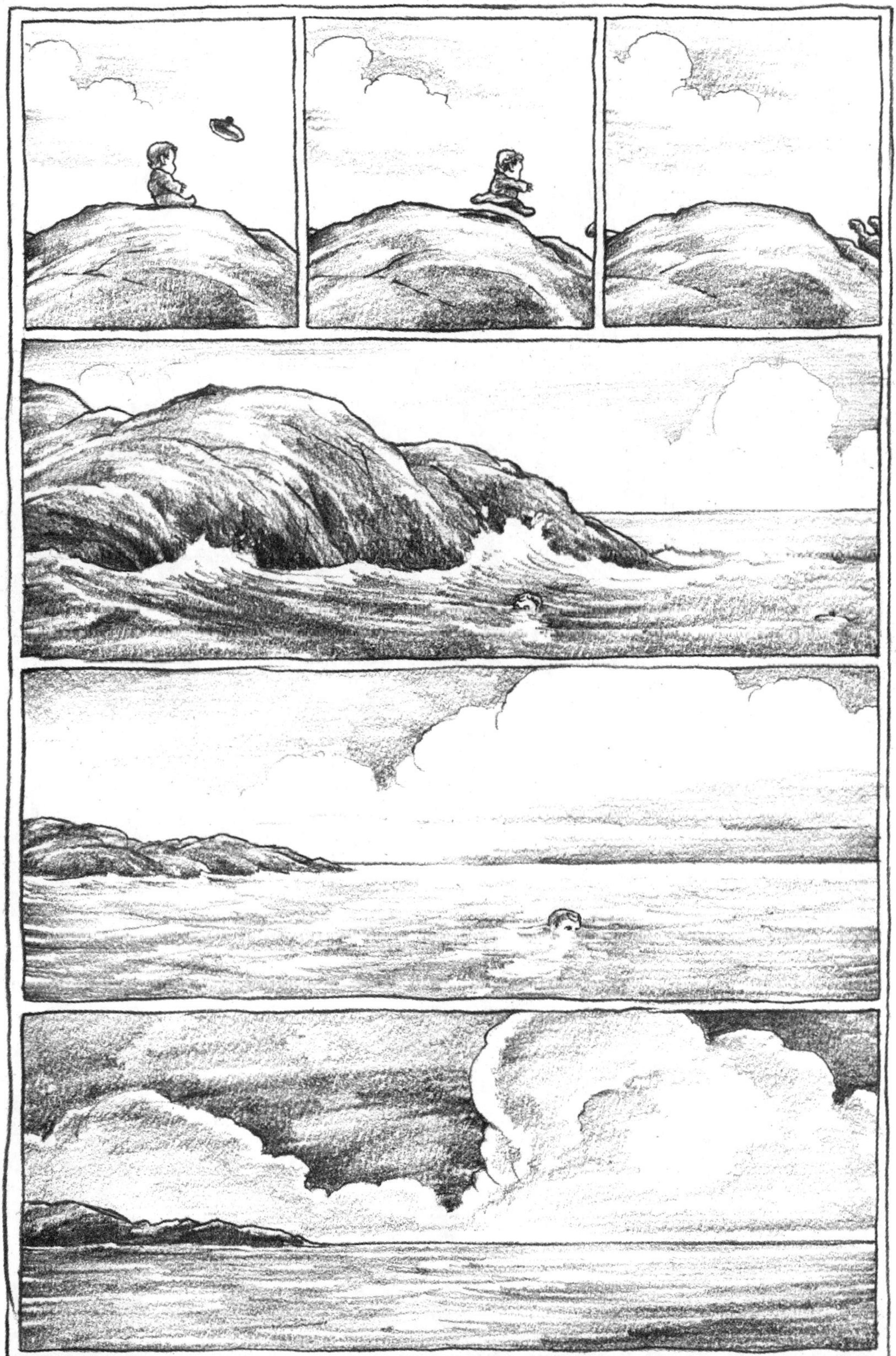

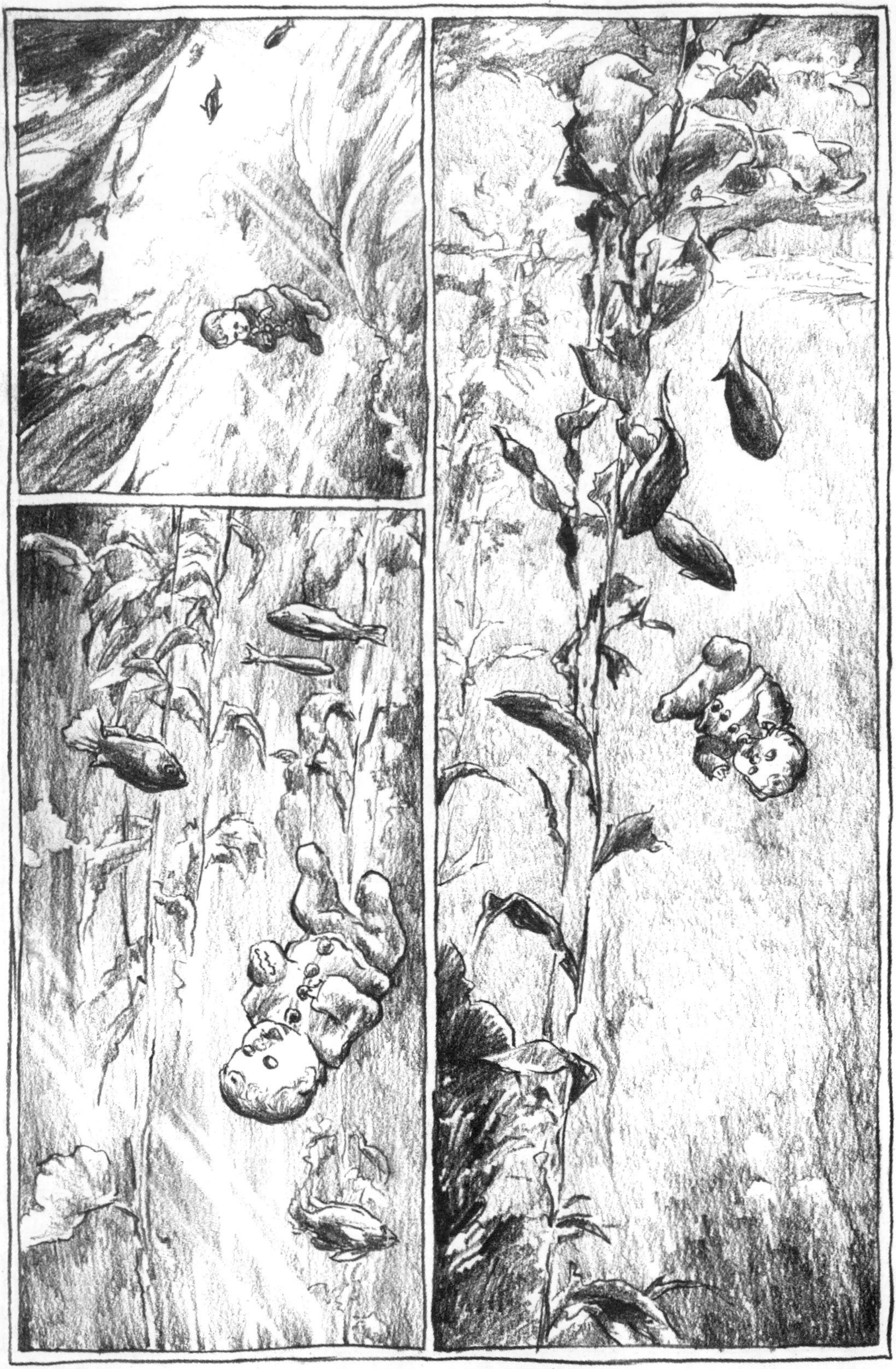

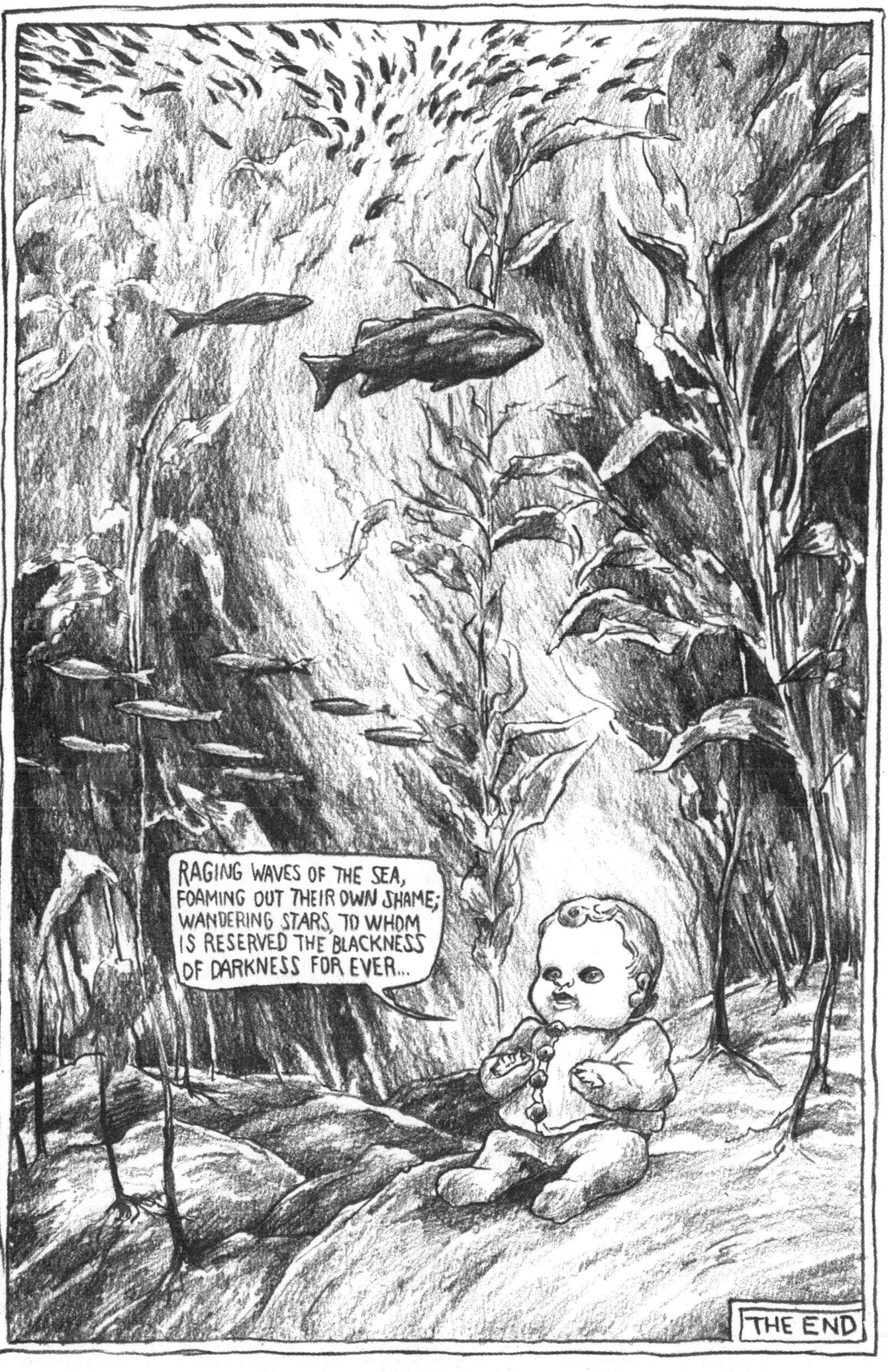
RAGING WAVES OF THE SEA, FOAMING OUT THEIR OWN SHAME; WANDERING STARS, TO WHOM IS RESERVED THE BLACKNESS OF DARKNESS FOR EVER...
THE END

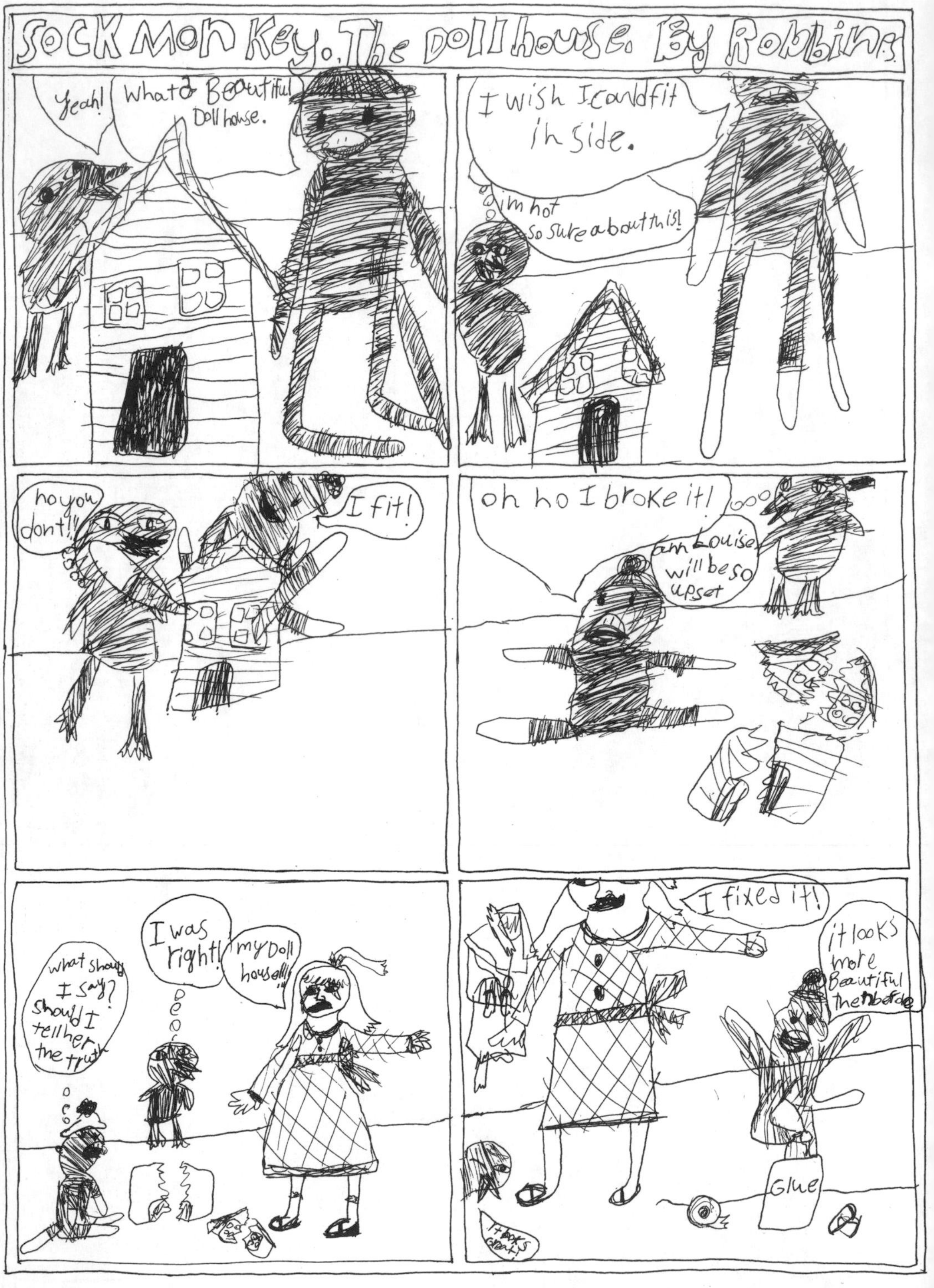
Sock Monkey. The Doll house. By Robbins
Yeah!
What a Beautiful Doll house.
I wish I could fit in side.
im not so sure about this!
no you dont!!
I fit!
oh no I broke it!
am Louise will be so upset
what should I say? should I tell her the truth
I was right!
my Doll house!!!
I fixed it!
it looks more Beautiful then before
Glue
It looks Great!

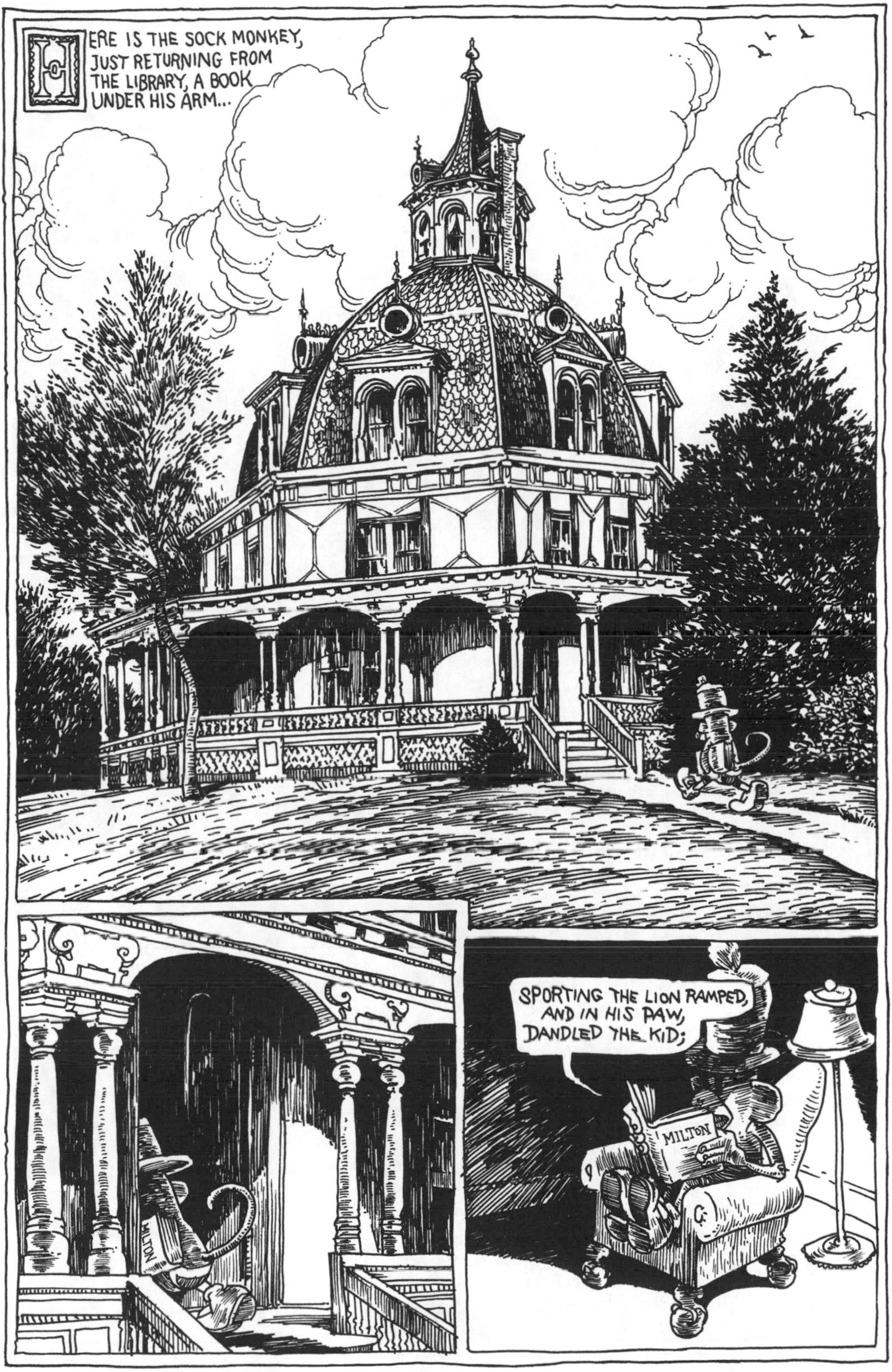
HERE IS THE SOCK MONKEY, JUST RETURNING FROM THE LIBRARY, A BOOK UNDER HIS ARM...
MILTON
SPORTING THE LION RAMPED, AND IN HIS PAW, DANDLED THE KID;
MILTON

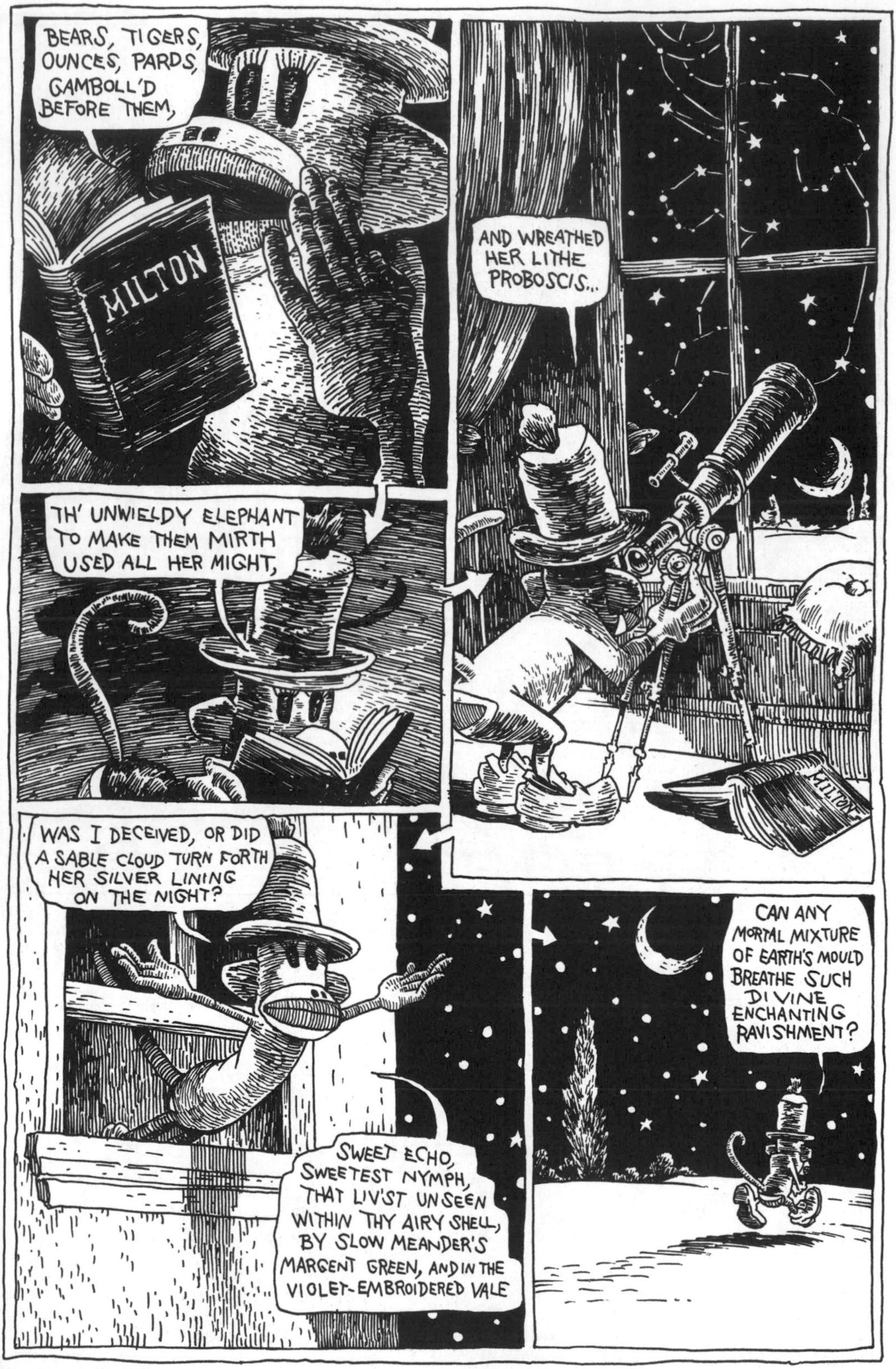
BEARS, TIGERS, OUNCES, PARDS, GAMBOLL'D BEFORE THEM,
MILTON
TH' UNWIELDY ELEPHANT TO MAKE THEM MIRTH USED ALL HER MIGHT,
AND WREATHED HER LITHE PROBOSCIS...
MILTON
WAS I DECEIVED, OR DID A SABLE CLOUD TURN FORTH HER SILVER LINING ON THE NIGHT?
SWEET ECHO, SWEETEST NYMPH, THAT LIV'ST UNSEEN WITHIN THY AIRY SHELL, BY SLOW MEANDER'S MARGENT GREEN, AND IN THE VIOLET-EMBROIDERED VALE
CAN ANY MORTAL MIXTURE OF EARTH'S MOULD BREATHE SUCH DIVINE ENCHANTING RAVISHMENT?

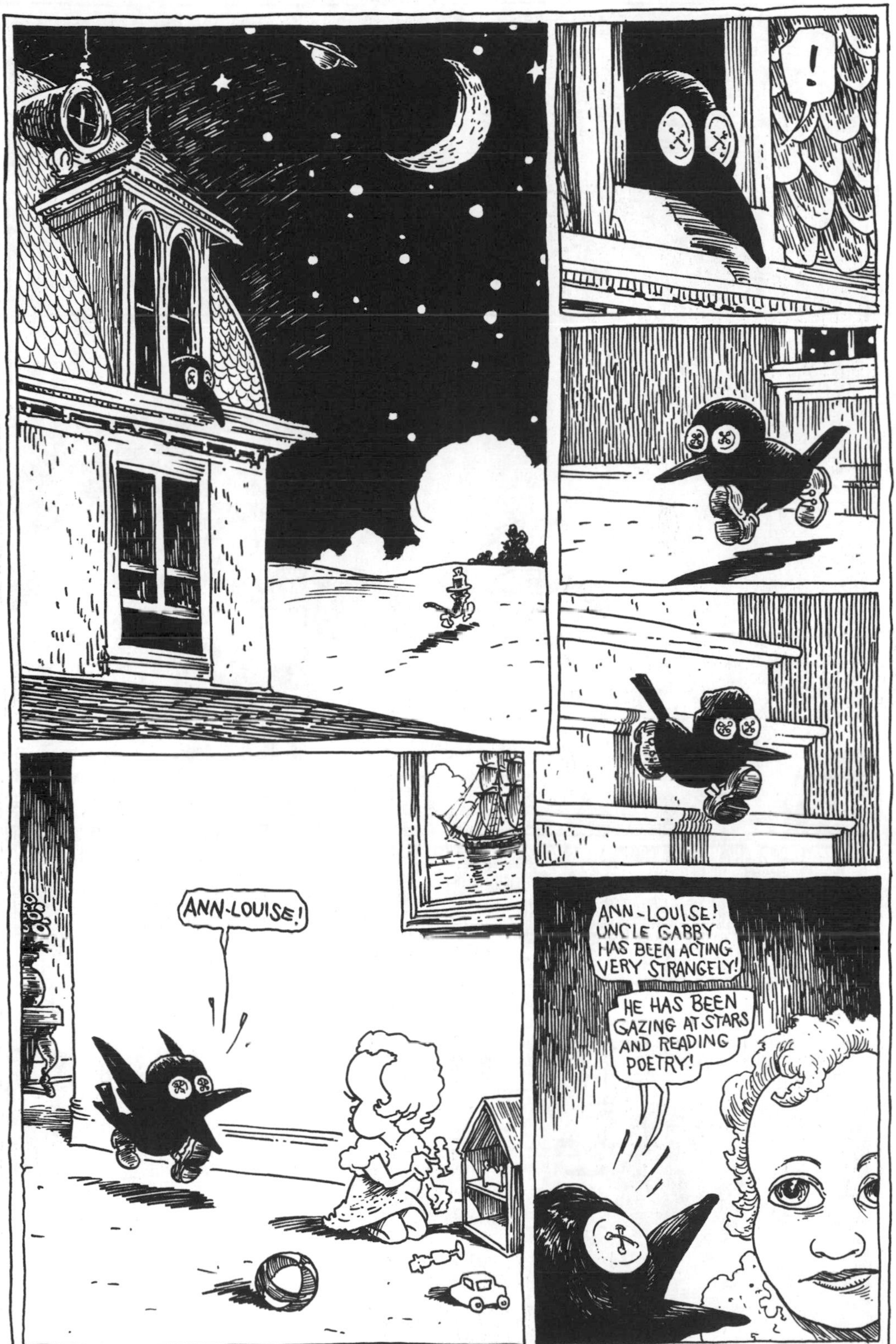
!
ANN-LOUISE!
ANN-LOUISE! UNCLE GABBY HAS BEEN ACTING VERY STRANGELY!
HE HAS BEEN GAZING AT STARS AND READING POETRY!

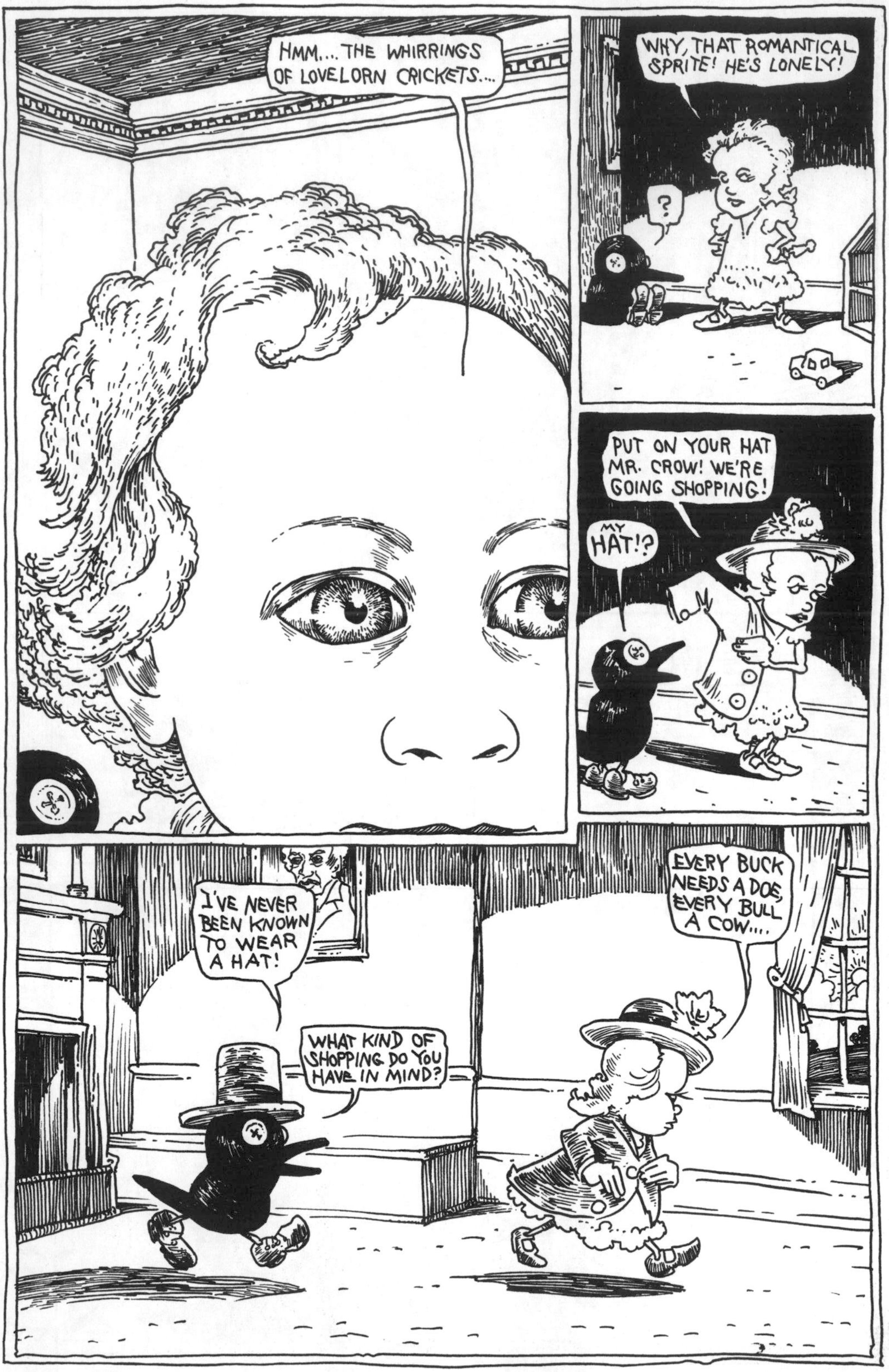

HMM.... THE WHIRRINGS OF LOVELORN CRICKETS....
WHY, THAT ROMANTICAL SPRITE! HE'S LONELY!
?
PUT ON YOUR HAT MR. CROW! WE'RE GOING SHOPPING!
MY HAT!?
I'VE NEVER BEEN KNOWN TO WEAR A HAT!
WHAT KIND OF SHOPPING DO YOU HAVE IN MIND?
EVERY BUCK NEEDS A DOE, EVERY BULL A COW....

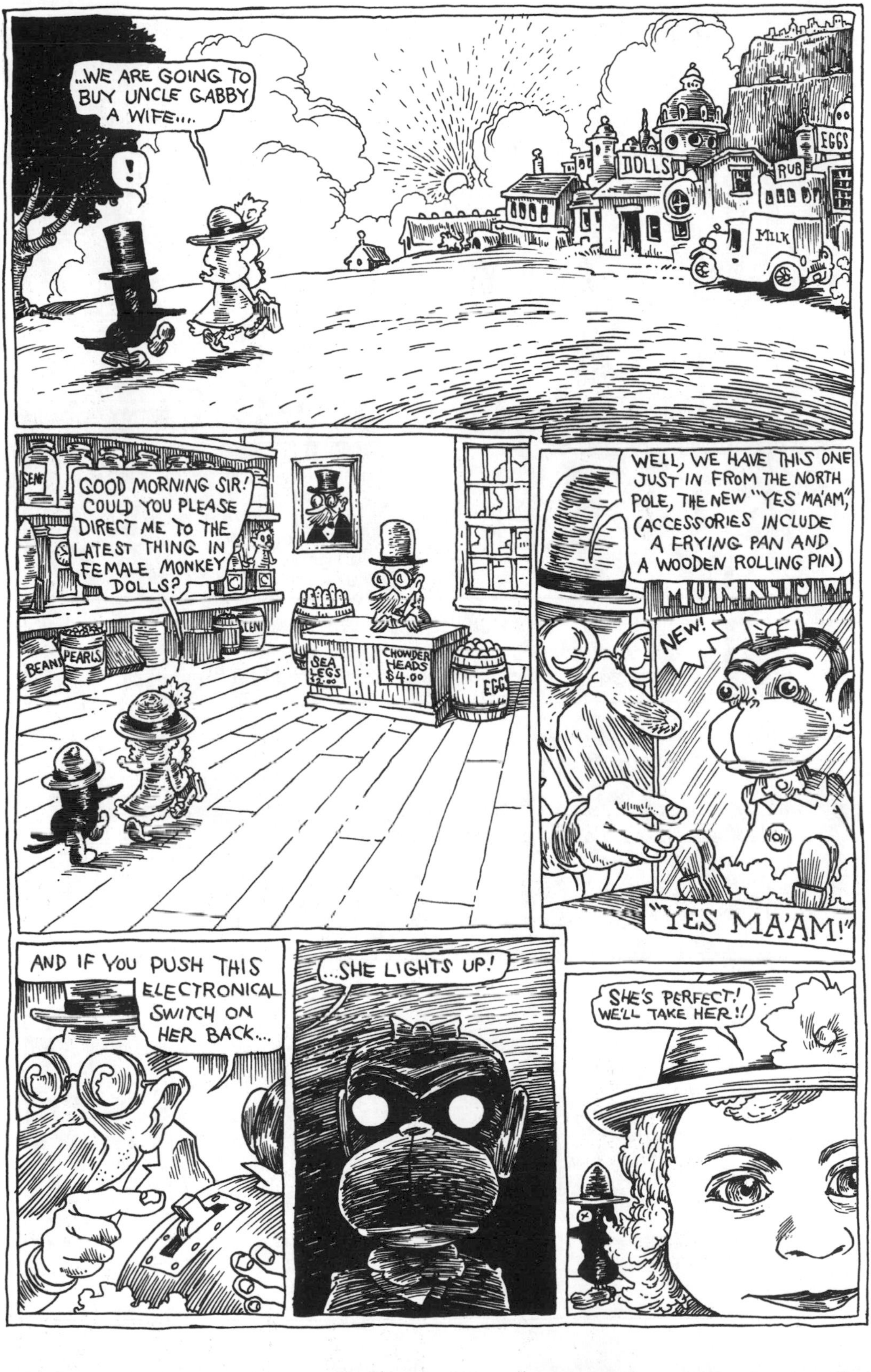
...WE ARE GOING TO BUY UNCLE GABBY A WIFE....
!
DOLLS
RUB
EGGS
MILK
SENF
GOOD MORNING SIR! COULD YOU PLEASE DIRECT ME TO THE LATEST THING IN FEMALE MONKEY DOLLS?
BEANS
PEARLS
SEA LEGS
CHOWDER HEADS $4.00
EGGS
WELL, WE HAVE THIS ONE JUST IN FROM THE NORTH POLE, THE NEW "YES MA'AM," (ACCESSORIES INCLUDE A FRYING PAN AND A WOODEN ROLLING PIN)
NEW!
"YES MA'AM!"
AND IF YOU PUSH THIS ELECTRONICAL SWITCH ON HER BACK...
...SHE LIGHTS UP!
SHE'S PERFECT! WE'LL TAKE HER!!

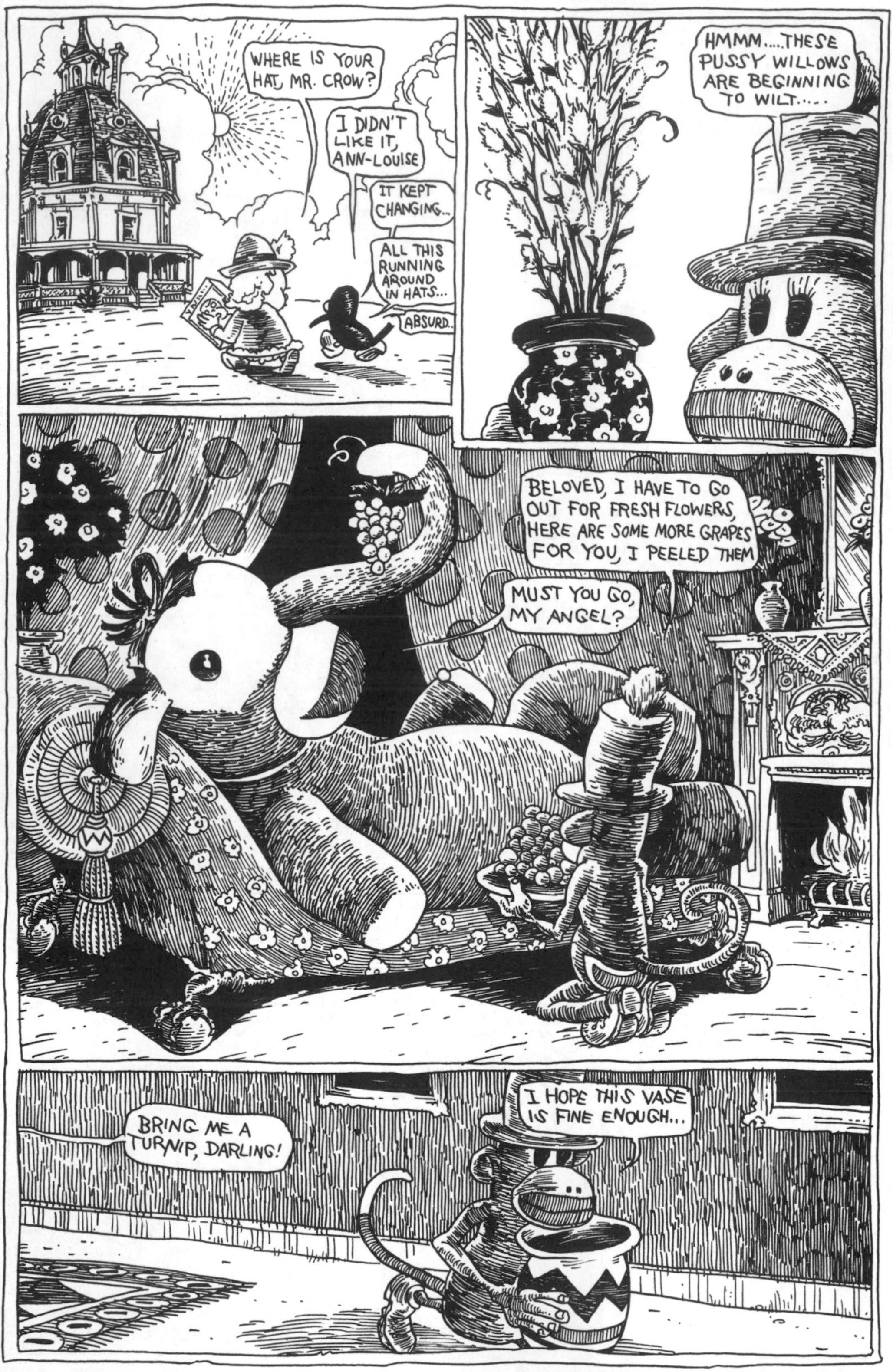
WHERE IS YOUR HAT, MR. CROW?
I DIDN'T LIKE IT, ANN-LOUISE
IT KEPT CHANGING...
ALL THIS RUNNING AROUND IN HATS...
ABSURD...
HMMM.....THESE PUSSY WILLOWS ARE BEGINNING TO WILT.....
BELOVED, I HAVE TO GO OUT FOR FRESH FLOWERS, HERE ARE SOME MORE GRAPES FOR YOU, I PEELED THEM
MUST YOU GO, MY ANGEL?
I HOPE THIS VASE IS FINE ENOUGH...
BRING ME A TURNIP, DARLING!

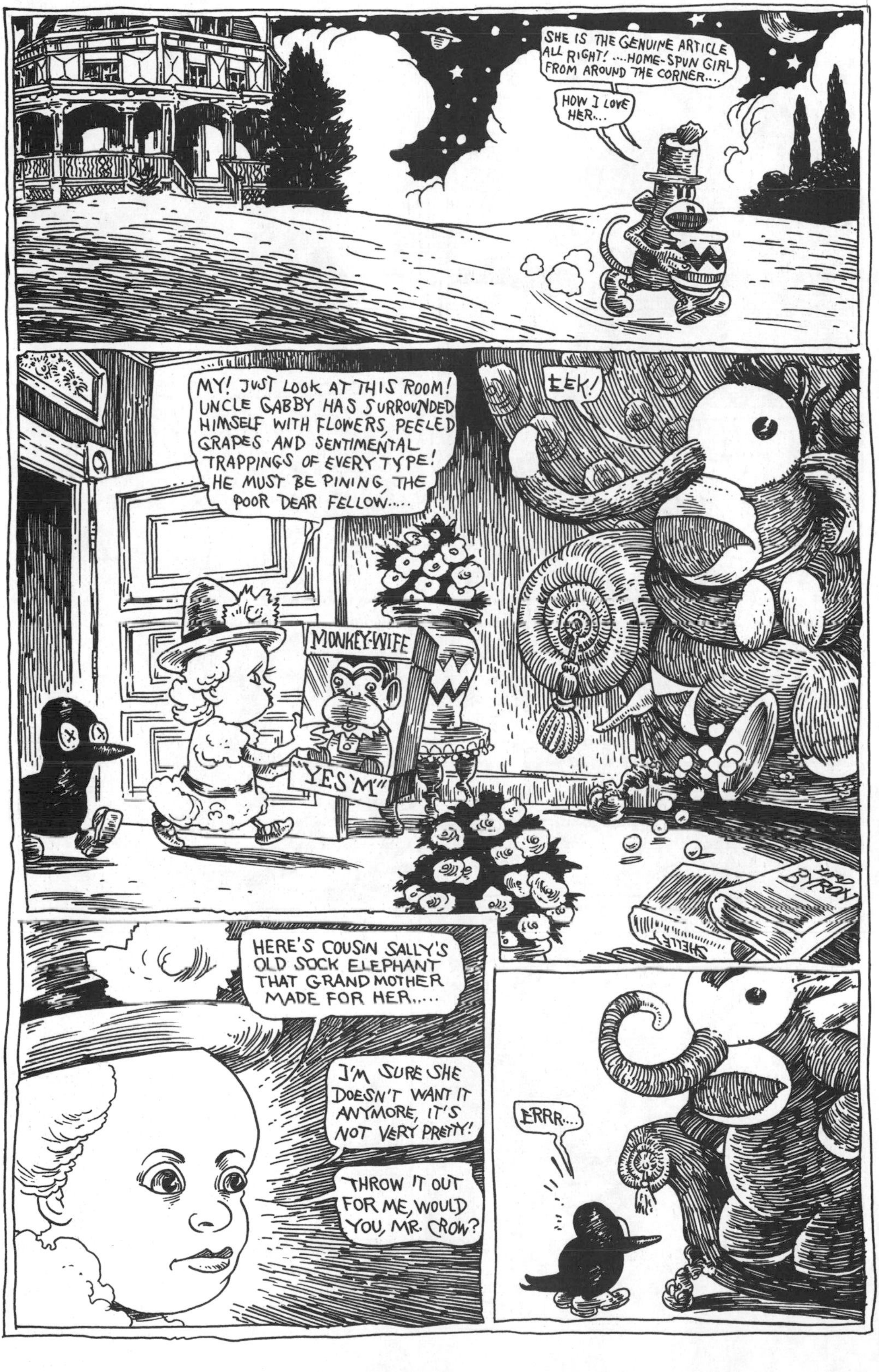
SHE IS THE GENUINE ARTICLE ALL RIGHT! ....HOME-SPUN GIRL FROM AROUND THE CORNER....
HOW I LOVE HER...
MY! JUST LOOK AT THIS ROOM! UNCLE GABBY HAS SURROUNDED HIMSELF WITH FLOWERS, PEELED GRAPES AND SENTIMENTAL TRAPPINGS OF EVERY TYPE! HE MUST BE PINING, THE POOR DEAR FELLOW.....
EEK!
MONKEY-WIFE
"YES'M"
BYRON
SHELLEY
HERE'S COUSIN SALLY'S OLD SOCK ELEPHANT THAT GRAND MOTHER MADE FOR HER.....
I'M SURE SHE DOESN'T WANT IT ANYMORE, IT'S NOT VERY PRETTY!
THROW IT OUT FOR ME, WOULD YOU, MR. CROW?
ERRR...

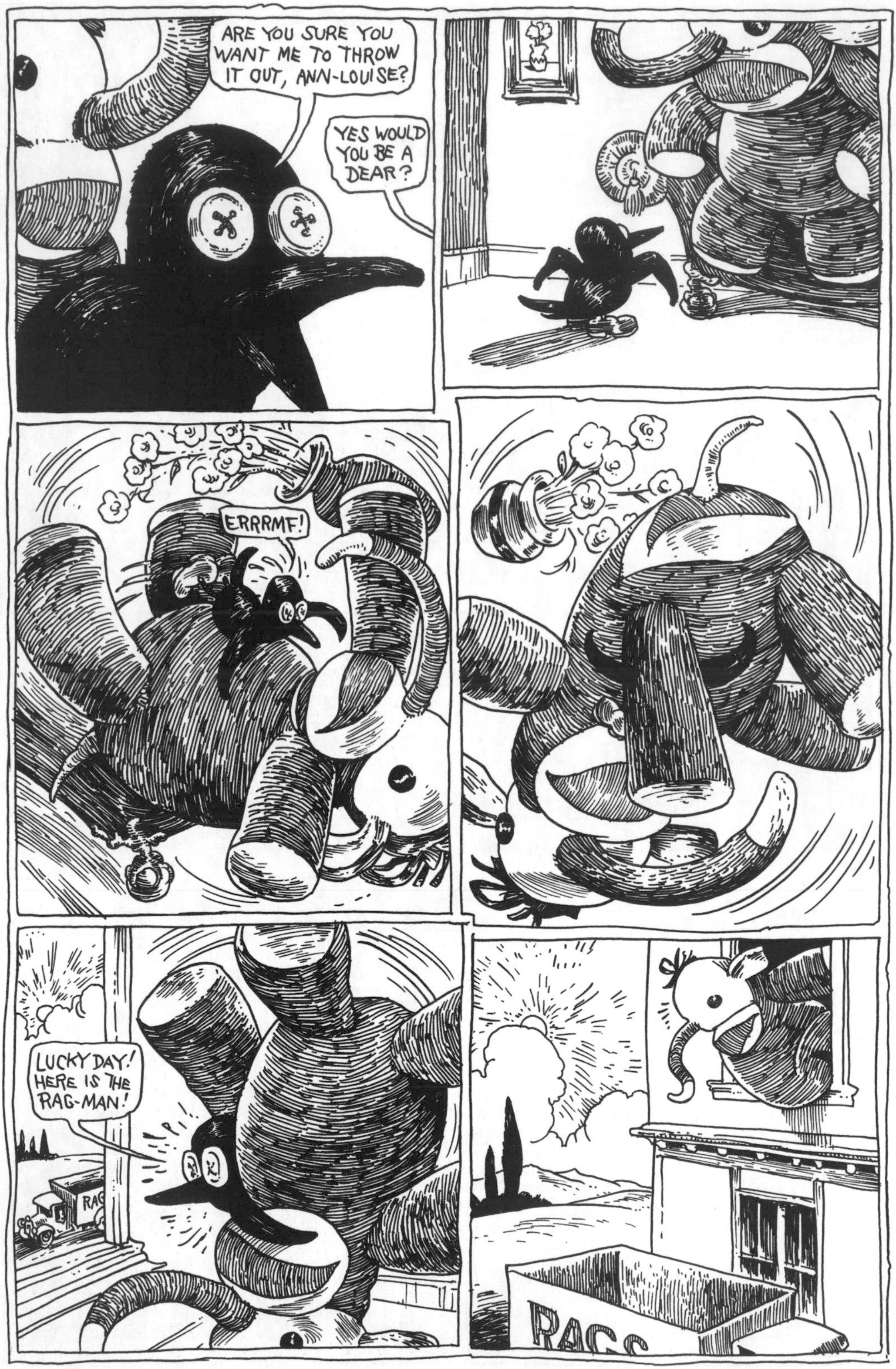

ARE YOU SURE YOU WANT ME TO THROW IT OUT, ANN-LOUISE?
YES WOULD YOU BE A DEAR?
ERRRMF!
LUCKY DAY! HERE IS THE RAG-MAN!
RAGS

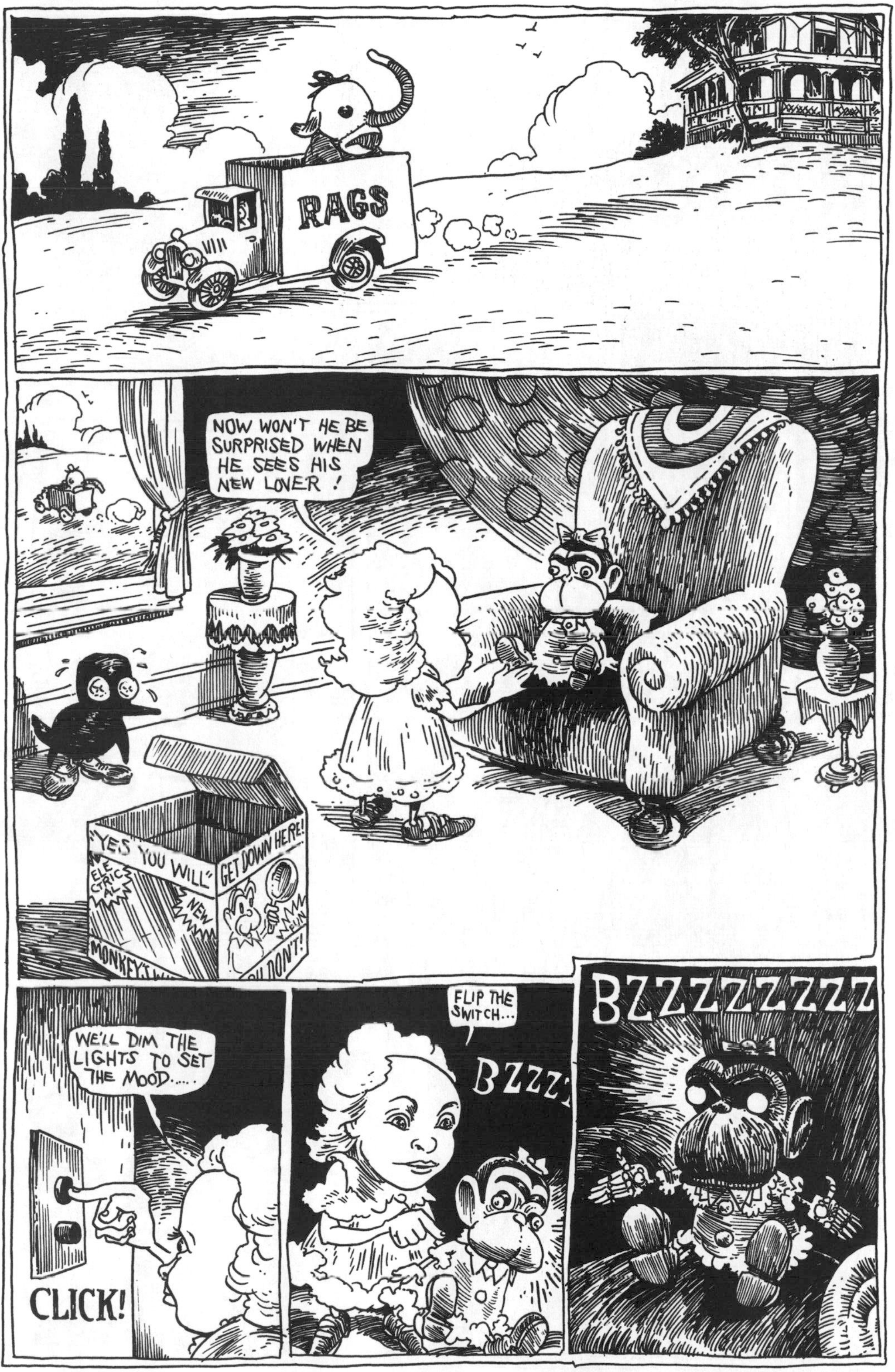
RAGS
NOW WON'T HE BE SURPRISED WHEN HE SEES HIS NEW LOVER !
"YES YOU WILL"
ELECTRICAL
NEW
GET DOWN HERE!
FUN
DON'T!
WE'LL DIM THE LIGHTS TO SET THE MOOD.....
CLICK!
FLIP THE SWITCH...
BZZZ
BZZZZZZZZ

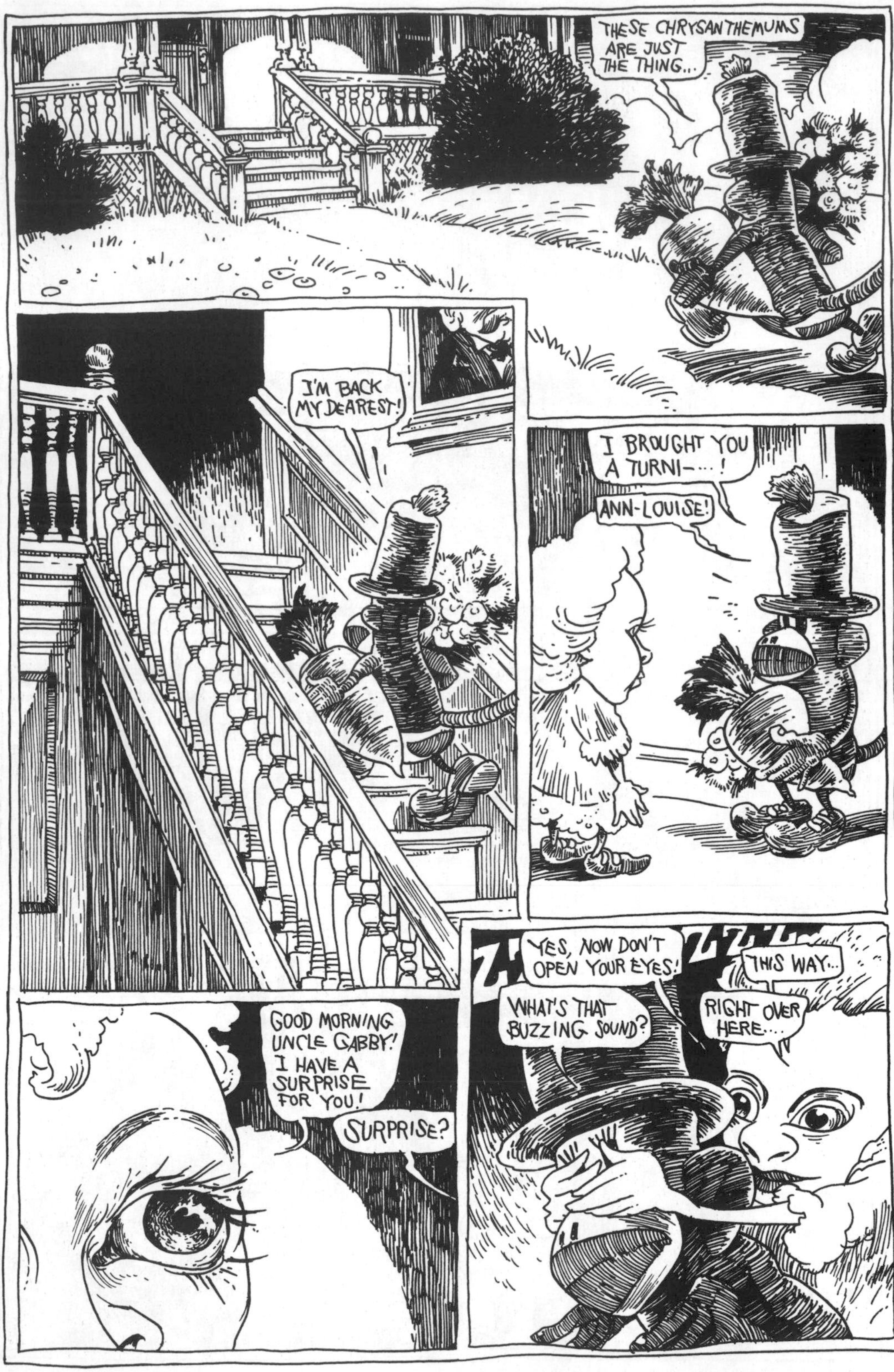
THESE CHRYSANTHEMUMS ARE JUST THE THING...
I'M BACK MY DEAREST!
I BROUGHT YOU A TURNI-...!
ANN-LOUISE!
GOOD MORNING UNCLE GABBY! I HAVE A SURPRISE FOR YOU!
SURPRISE?
YES, NOW DON'T OPEN YOUR EYES!
WHAT'S THAT BUZZING SOUND?
THIS WAY...
RIGHT OVER HERE...

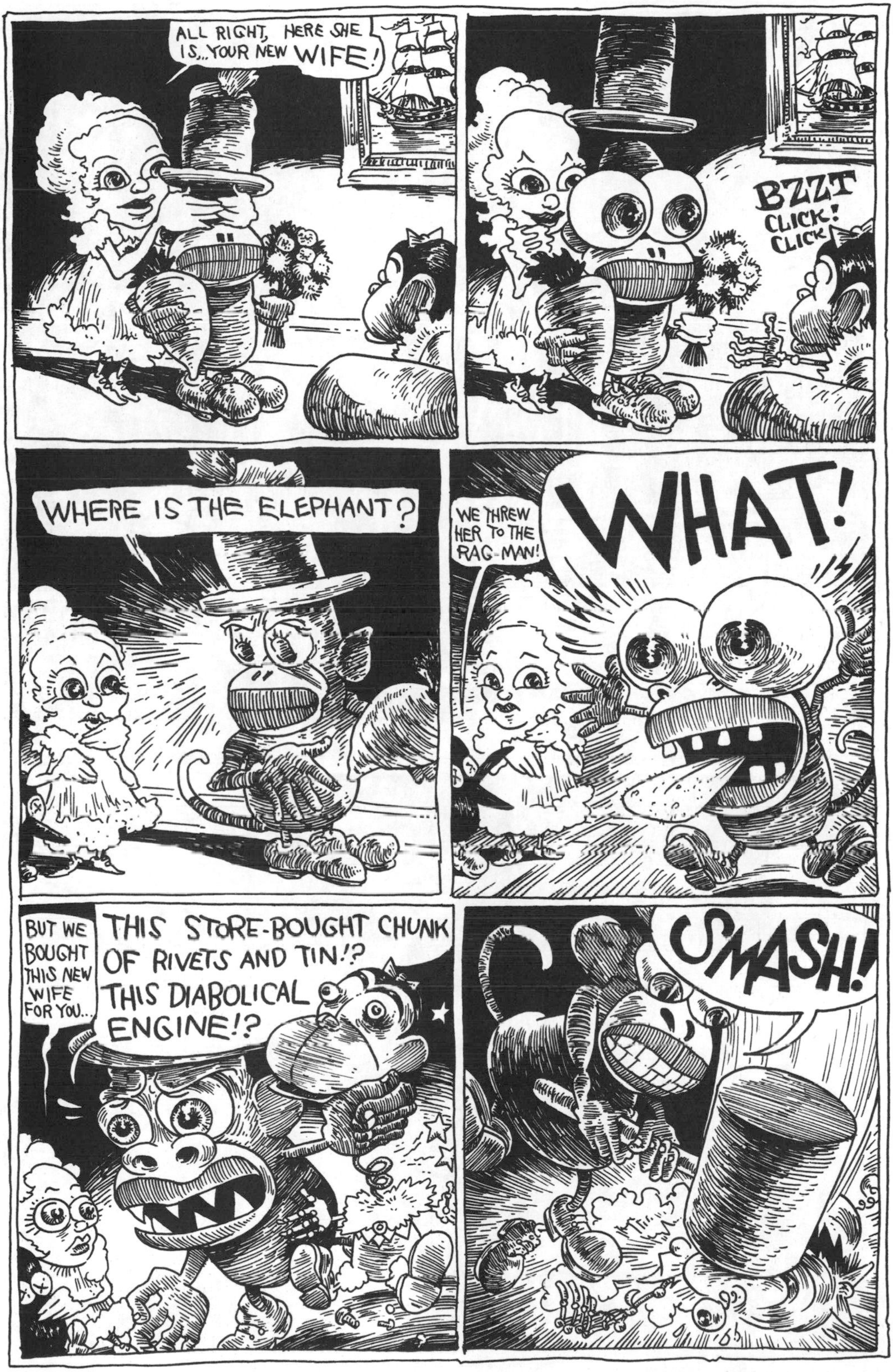
ALL RIGHT, HERE SHE IS... YOUR NEW WIFE!
BZZT
CLICK! CLICK!
WHERE IS THE ELEPHANT?
WE THREW HER TO THE RAG-MAN!
WHAT!
BUT WE BOUGHT THIS NEW WIFE FOR YOU...
THIS STORE-BOUGHT CHUNK OF RIVETS AND TIN!? THIS DIABOLICAL ENGINE!?
SMASH!

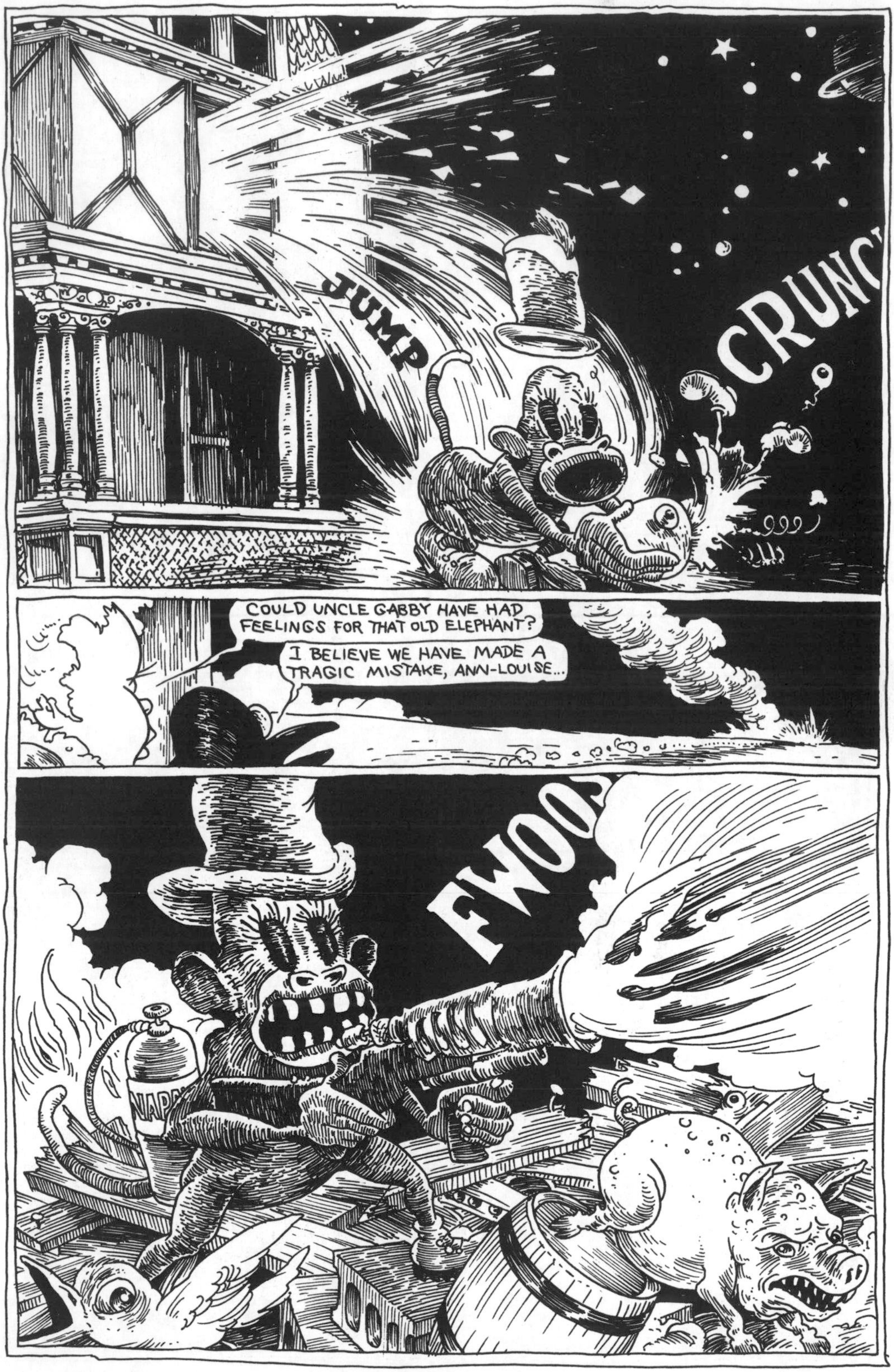
JUMP
CRUNC
COULD UNCLE GABBY HAVE HAD FEELINGS FOR THAT OLD ELEPHANT?
I BELIEVE WE HAVE MADE A TRAGIC MISTAKE, ANN-LOUISE...
FWOOS

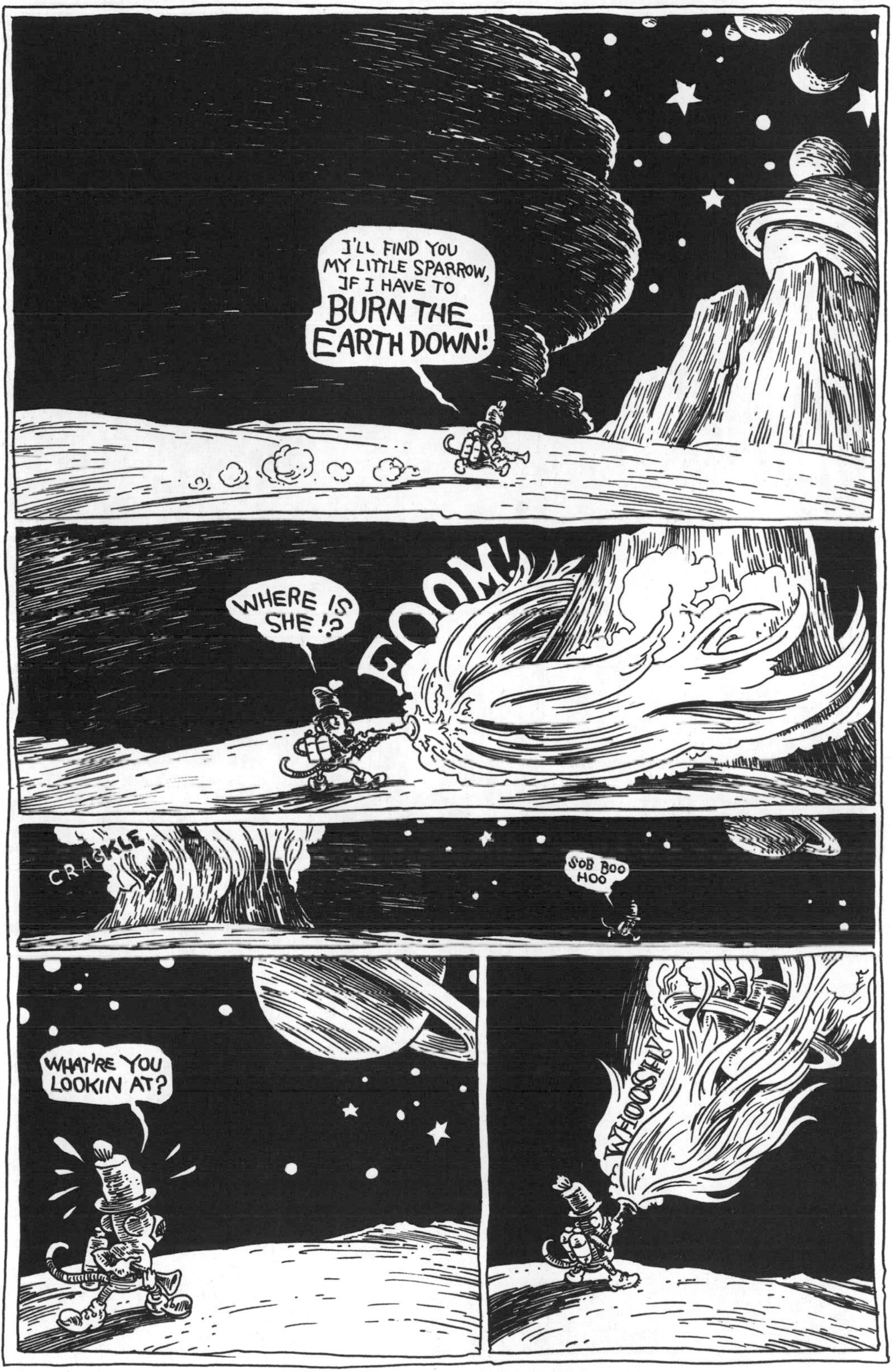
I'LL FIND YOU MY LITTLE SPARROW, IF I HAVE TO BURN THE EARTH DOWN!
WHERE IS SHE!?
FOOM!
CRACKLE
SOB BOO HOO
WHAT'RE YOU LOOKIN AT?
WHOOSH!

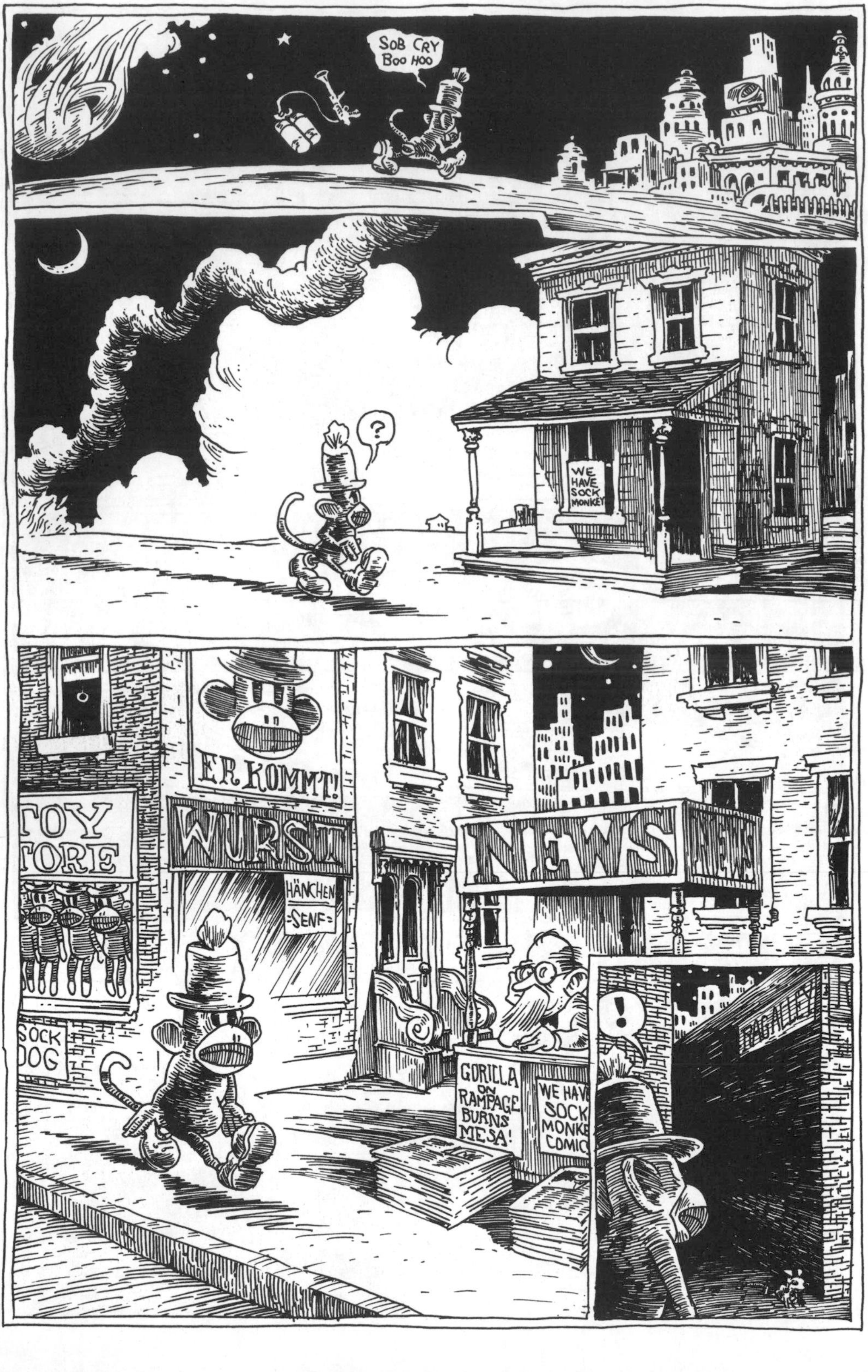

SOB CRY BOO HOO
?
WE HAVE SOCK MONKEY
ER KOMMT!
TOY
TORE
WURST
HÄNCHEN -SENF-
NEWS
NEWS
SOCK DOG
GORILLA ON RAMPAGE BURNS MESA!
WE HAV SOCK MONKE COMIC
!
RAG ALLEY

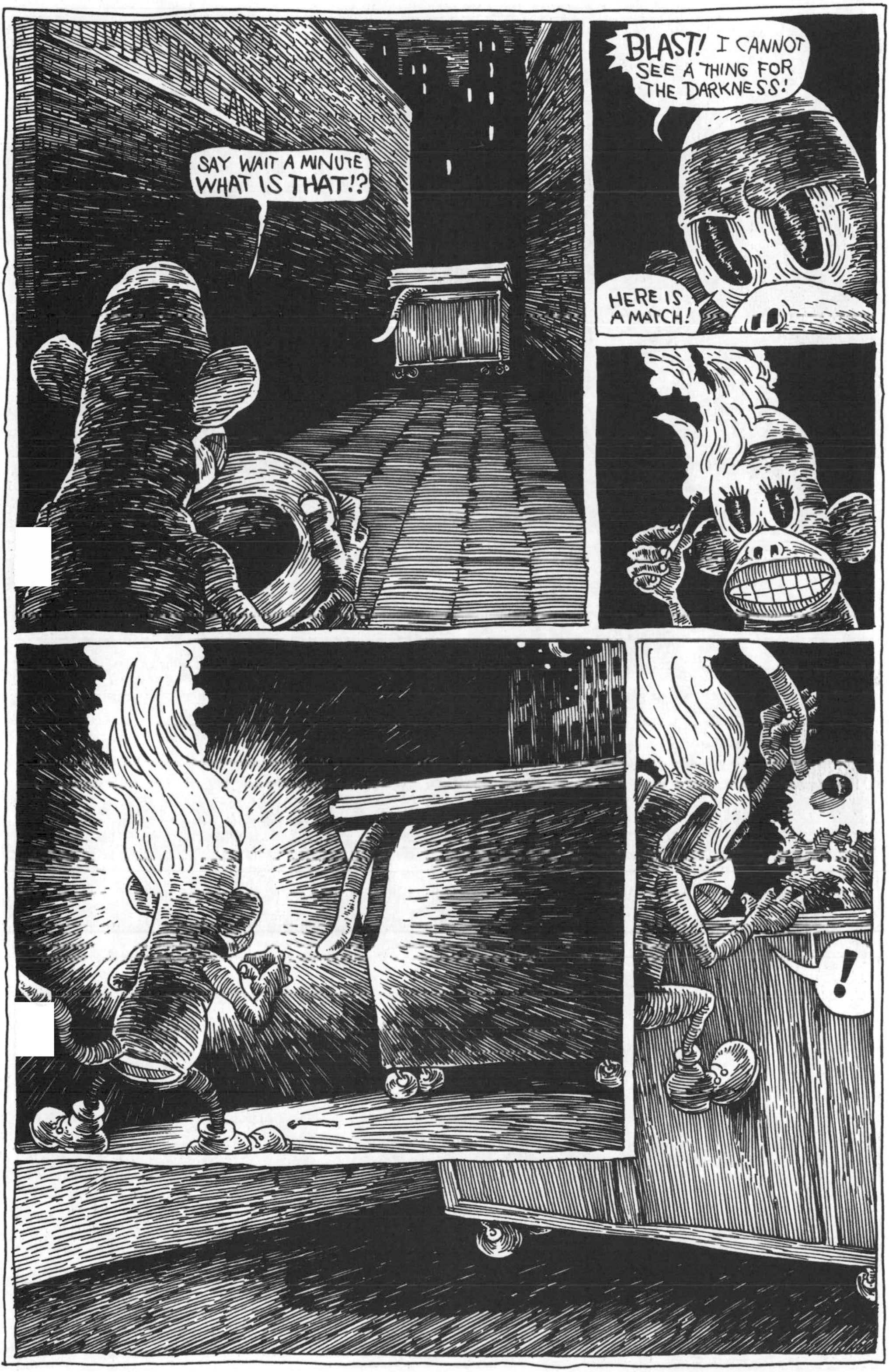
DUMPSTER LANE
SAY WAIT A MINUTE WHAT IS THAT!?
BLAST! I CANNOT SEE A THING FOR THE DARKNESS!
HERE IS A MATCH!
!

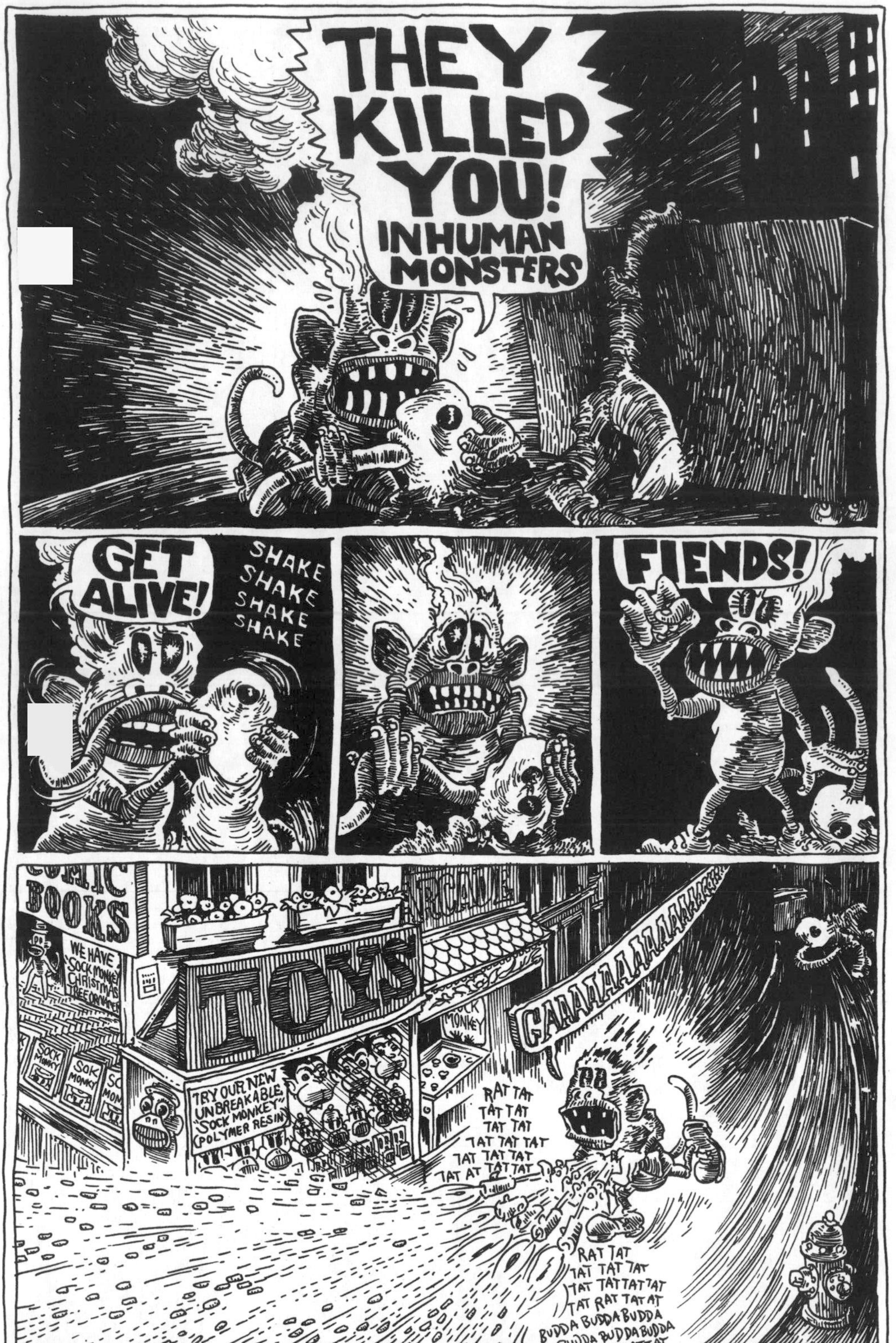
THEY KILLED YOU! INHUMAN MONSTERS
GET ALIVE!
SHAKE SHAKE SHAKE SHAKE
FIENDS!
COMIC BOOKS
WE HAVE SOCK MONKEY CHRISTMAS TREE ORNAMENTS
TOYS
SOCK MONKEY
SOCK MONKEY
SOK MONKEY
TRY OUR NEW UNBREAKABLE "SOCK MONKEY" POLYMER RESIN
GAAAAAAAAAAAAAAAHH
RAT TAT TAT TAT TAT TAT TAT TAT TAT TAT TAT TAT TAT AT TAT TAT
RAT TAT TAT TAT TAT TAT TAT TAT TAT TAT RAT TAT AT BUDDA BUDDA BUDDA BUDDA BUDDA BUDDA

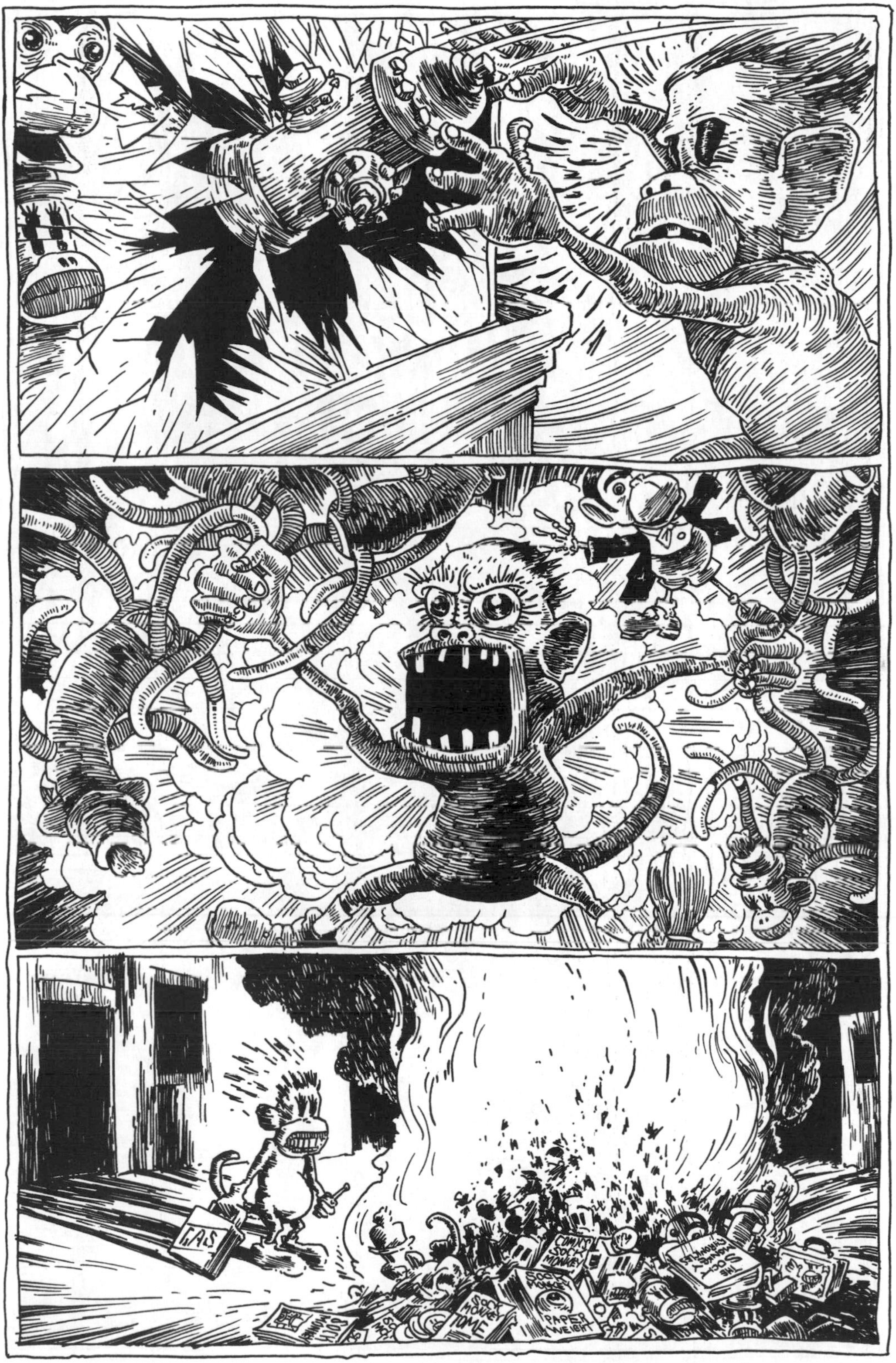

GAS
COMIX SOCK MONKEY
THE SOCK MONKEY CHRONICLES
SOCK MONKEY TOME
SOCK MONKEY PAPER WEIGHT

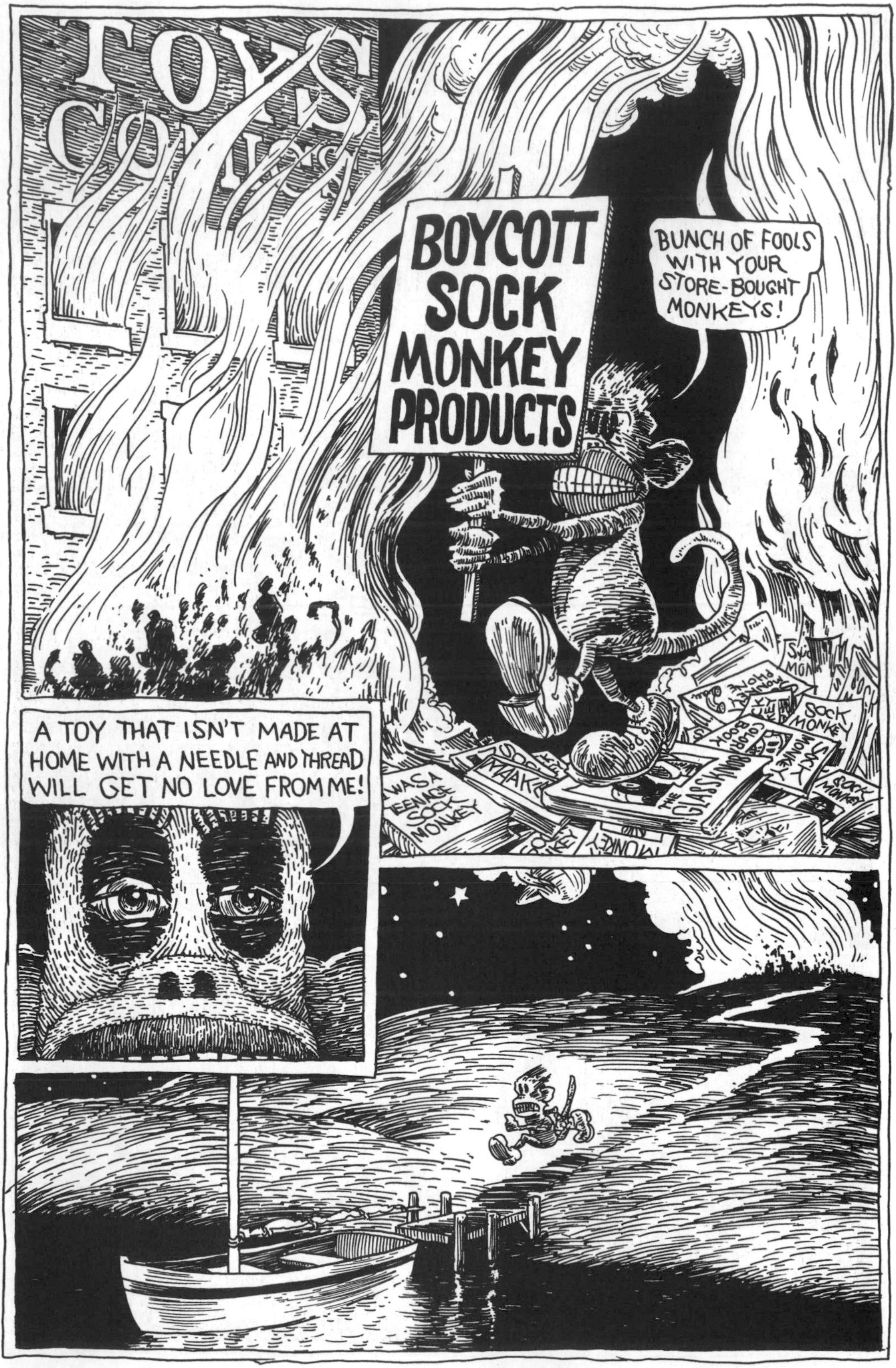

TOYS
COMICS
BOYCOTT SOCK MONKEY PRODUCTS
BUNCH OF FOOLS WITH YOUR STORE-BOUGHT MONKEYS!
A TOY THAT ISN'T MADE AT HOME WITH A NEEDLE AND THREAD WILL GET NO LOVE FROM ME!
SOCK MONKEY
SOCK MONKEY

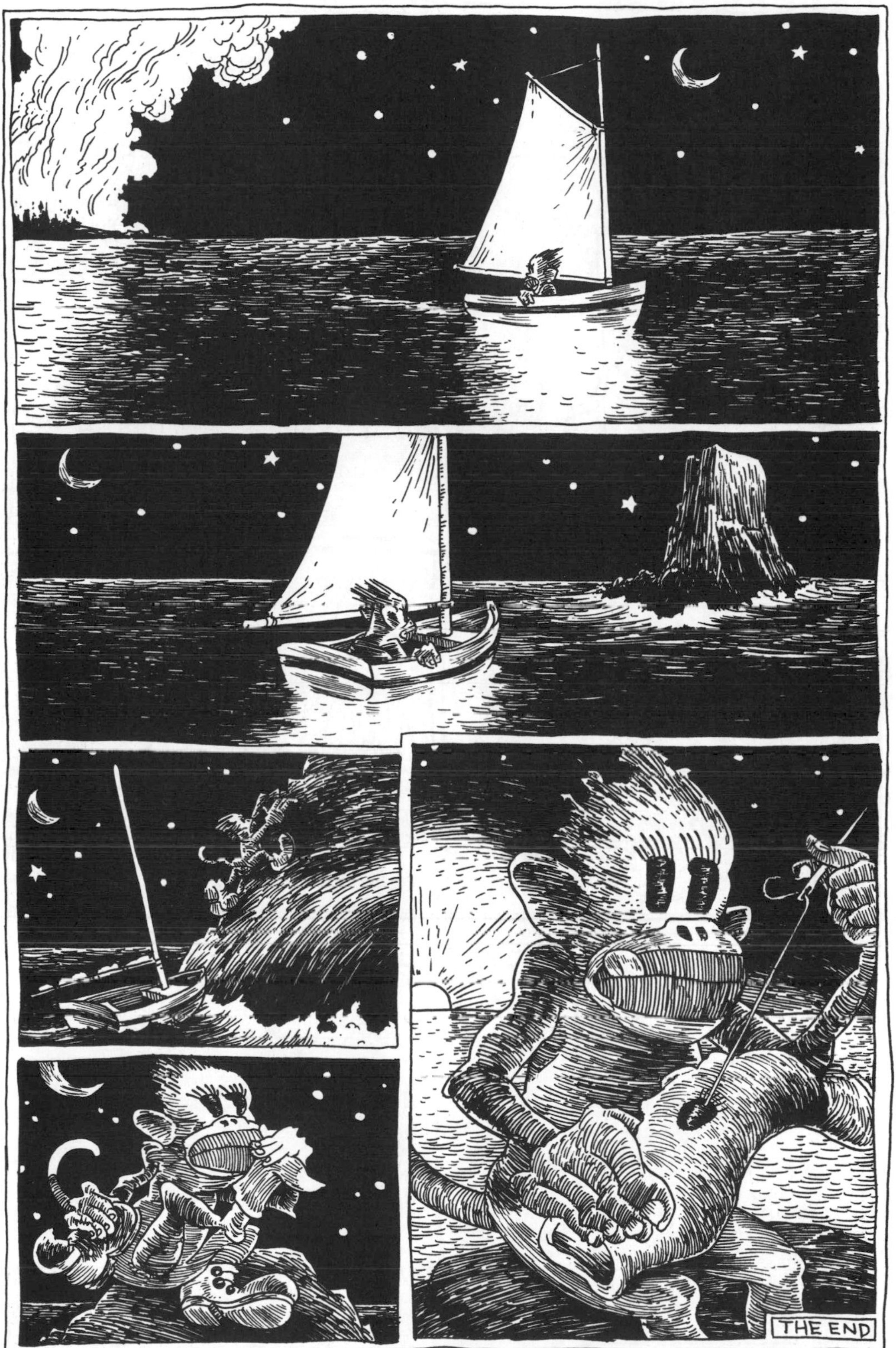
THE END

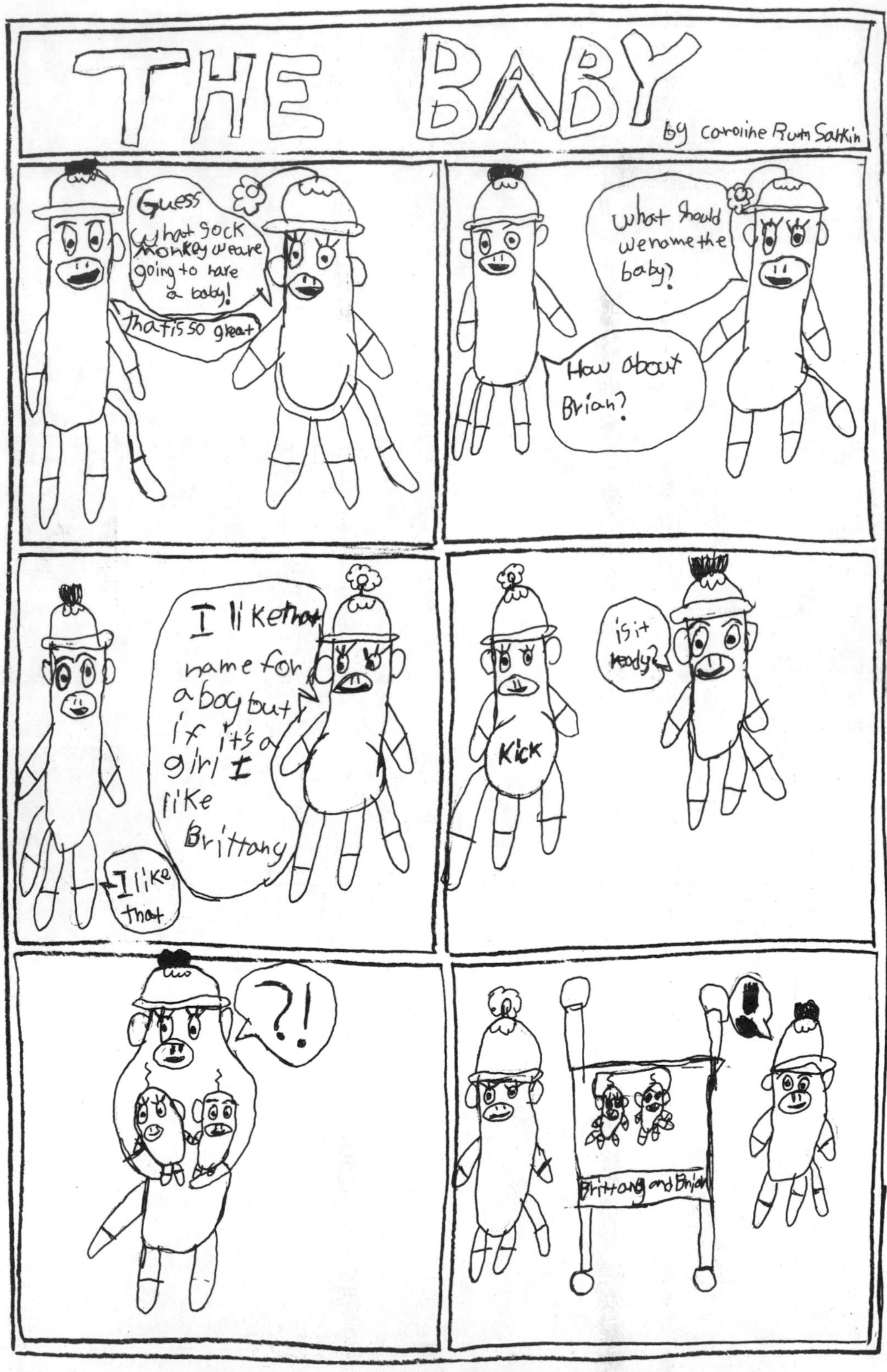
THE BABY
by Caroline Ruth Satkin
Guess what sock monkey we are going to have a baby!
That is so great
What should we name the baby?
How about Brian?
I like that name for a boy but if it's a girl I like Brittany
I like that
Kick
Is it ready?
?!
Brittany and Brian